To: gigi

fr: Cheryl

May This book
help you with your
walk with God,
Jesus & the holy
Spirit!

God Bless you
on your Journey.

From
PASSOVER
to
PENTECOST

From
PASSOVER
to
PENTECOST

CYNTHIA SCHNEIDER

CHARISMA
HOUSE

From Passover to Pentecost by Cynthia Schneider
Published by Charisma House
Charisma Media/Charisma House Book Group
600 Rinehart Road, Lake Mary, Florida 32746

Scripture quotations marked TLV are taken from the Tree of Life
Translation of the Bible. Copyright © 2015 by The Messianic Jewish
Family Bible Society.

Visit the author's website at https://discoveringthejewishjesus
.com/.

Library of Congress Cataloging-in-Publication Data:
An application to register this book for cataloging has been submitted
to the Library of Congress.
International Standard Book Number: 978-1-62999-924-1
E-book ISBN: 978-1-62999-925-8

21 22 23 24 25 — 9 8 7 6 5 4 3 2 1
Printed in the United States of America

CONTENTS

ACKNOWLEDGMENTS

IGIVE MY HIGHEST praise and honor to my faithful Father God, my beloved Yeshua, and my constant Comforter, the Holy Spirit, to whom I dedicate this work.

I thank my Lord for my heavenly minded husband, Rabbi Kirt A. Schneider, who has been used of the Father to answer my prayers and transform my life. May we always be bound together in love and dedicated to running the race to the end for Yeshua's eternal glory.

I sing praises to the Lord for my cherished children, their husbands, and their children. Truly God's great and perfect love, beauty, grace, and joy are revealed to me through their lives. I thank my daughters for their love, patience, and grace toward me throughout their lives. May our faithful Father complete the good work He has begun through this family dedicated unto Him.

I thank and praise God for the beloved body of Messiah—my precious sisters and brothers, both by blood and by the Spirit, who have *truly* been bound together with me through the love and blood of Jesus. They have been great armor bearers, supporting me through their love, prayers, and words. I have been greatly blessed to experience Father's family on earth, knit together in Yeshua's love and unified by the Holy Spirit. This beautiful, imperfect family, the body of Messiah, brings Father's multifaceted love, grace, and strength into the earth. May we continue to stay bound together in Yeshua's love and finish this race for Yeshua and His kingdom!

O Lord, You who have begun this work, breathe Your Spirit into each person who reads the following pages. Speak to and freely fellowship with Your bride!

INTRODUCTION

A Season of Hope and Breakthrough

When the day of Pentecost came, they were all together in one place. Suddenly a sound like the blowing of a violent wind came from heaven and filled the whole house where they were sitting. They saw what seemed to be tongues of fire that separated and came to rest on each of them. All of them were filled with the Holy Spirit and began to speak in other tongues as the Spirit enabled them.

—ACTS 2:1–4, NIV

T HE DAY OF Pentecost is often viewed as the birth of the Christian church because the number of believers exploded after the Holy Spirit descended upon those who gathered in the Upper Room. But Pentecost existed long before Yeshua (Jesus) walked the earth.

Pentecost (Greek for *fiftieth*) refers to the Feast or Festival of Weeks (Shavuot in Hebrew). It is celebrated seven weeks after the first day of Passover (the fiftieth day from Passover). In ancient Israel it was a time of thanking God for His provision and celebrating the firstfruits of harvest. "You shall celebrate the Feast of Weeks, that is, the first fruits of the wheat harvest, and the Feast of Ingathering at the turn of the year" (Exod. 34:22).

The Jewish feasts and celebrations outlined in the Torah (the first five books of the Bible) are given to God's children to help us stay focused on Him as our source and strength. He knew that we as mortal vessels in a fallen world are easily distracted and enticed away from relationship with Him. He also knew that we must be in relationship with Him to receive the fullness of His life and beauty. The holy days and celebrations throughout the Hebrew calendar help God's people remember Him and look to Him in humility, love, and appreciation of His faithfulness. These holy days of the Lord also teach us the key truths of redemption and help us anticipate and receive Yeshua's new good gifts.

This book will take you on a journey in hopes that you will encounter the fire and wind of the Holy Spirit that was released on the day of Pentecost. It is designed to help you focus on knowing, following, and worshipping the Lord with great expectation and trust in Him, bringing new life and provision in the days ahead.

As Leviticus 23:15–16 instructs, God's people would count the days from Passover (the day the Lamb was sacrificed; see related sidebar) to Pentecost: "You shall also count for yourselves from the day after the sabbath [the Passover Sabbath], from the day when you brought in the sheaf of the wave offering; there shall be seven complete sabbaths. You shall count fifty days to the day after the seventh sabbath; then you shall present a new grain offering to the Lord." This practice of counting the time between Passover and Pentecost continues today. It represents keeping a heart of thanksgiving for the Lord's deliverance and provision and also creates great anticipation for more of what the Lord will give to bless and keep His people in the future.

Over time Pentecost (Shavuot) became a time to remember the giving of the Law of Moses at Mount Sinai, and the Jewish people spend the weeks leading up to Pentecost recalling this epic God encounter that changed history. In a similar way, for followers of Messiah Jesus, this time between Passover and Pentecost presents an opportunity to recall the first believers' faith to wait in the Upper Room for the promise of the Father (Luke 24:49): *the baptism of the Holy Spirit.*

On the day of Pentecost, the Scripture says, the Spirit of God descended from heaven like a violent, rushing wind and rested as tongues of fire on the believers gathered in the Upper Room. The promised Comforter had come, and not only would He guide those gathered into all truth; He would actually fill them with Himself. Take a minute to really think about that. The very Spirit of God not only filled the room but *inhabited* those who put their faith in Jesus as Messiah.

The blessed and beautiful truth is that the Holy Spirit

still makes His habitation among us, filling us with His power, truth, and love today. He guides and teaches us, revealing the Father's love, grace, and mercy, causing us to experience His power and victory in our lives.

My prayer is that as you meditate on the scriptures and daily devotions, you will move progressively through the fifty days to encounter our almighty, saving God. He is high and lifted up in infinite, perfect love and holiness. And He stands in stark contrast to the weaknesses, imperfections, and brokenness found in our daily lives. Seeing ourselves for who we are apart from our Creator—broken clay vessels filled with the spirit of this world and lacking the wisdom, power, or authority to love or receive love perfectly—is an important part of the process of becoming free and whole in Jesus.

The devotions in *From Passover to Pentecost* position you to encounter Father God for salvation, deep healing, and wholeness. As you daily ask Jesus to take all the darkness plaguing your life into Himself, sin's power against you is destroyed and you gain His powerful joy, hope, and resurrection life. As you call upon the Holy Spirit's revelation over the next fifty days, may your heart and mind be transformed to reflect the heart and mind of Messiah Jesus, who sets you free!

The Blessing of Passover

Sin created a chasm between God and the people He made in His own image. Restoring the fellowship that was lost required the shedding of blood. In love, God created a system of substitutionary, sacrificial atonement (Lev. 17:11).

During Pharaoh's oppressive rule over the Jewish people in Egypt, God instructed His people to slaughter a lamb and place the blood over the doorposts of their homes. Done in faith, this sacrificial blood protected the Israelites from the judgment God was pouring out upon the Egyptians. God said: "When I see the blood, I will pass over you. No destructive plague will touch you when I strike Egypt" (Exod. 12:13, NIV). God instructed His people to forever remember and celebrate His protection and deliverance from oppression, which came through their Passover lamb (Lev. 23:4–5; Num. 9:2).

Yet the promised protection of the Passover lamb found its fulfillment in Messiah Jesus. Jesus told His disciples during the Passover celebration, "This is my blood of the covenant, which is poured out for many for the forgiveness of sins" (Matt. 26:28, NIV). The blood Jesus shed on the cross offers forgiveness, protection, and deliverance from sin and oppression once and for all. Beloved, the Father's love is revealed through the Passover. Christ, our Passover Lamb, has been sacrificed, *and our victory is secure in Him!*

Seek the Things Above

So we fix our eyes not on what is seen, but on what is unseen, since what is seen is temporary, but what is unseen is eternal.

—2 CORINTHIANS 4:18, NIV

A S WE SEEK things above, we also have to contend with the things below, and it is a constant challenge. Daily pressing needs and distractions hinder us from focusing on our unseen God.

As my husband and I travel in the United States and abroad, sharing the gospel through our ministry, Discovering the Jewish Jesus, I am continually seeking to stay in God's peace while also completing the mundane tasks of keeping our home clean and organized, making meals, doing laundry, and handling the responsibilities of the ministry with their various deadlines. After spending so much time warring in the spirit to get to the airport to travel to the next ministry engagement, I am often exhausted, overwhelmed, and fearful that I have forgotten an important detail. I feel far from perfect in my ability to make everything "perfect"!

But when I settle into my seat on the plane and relinquish all my failures and inadequacies to Yeshua, calling on *His* adequacy and perfection to cover my life, then the miracle begins to occur. Jesus washes away my inadequacies, and the Holy Spirit begins to fill my heart and mind with His hope and vision for my life. As the plane ascends, I get a new perspective. I look down from the window and find that all the hustle and bustle below starts fading away. My vision changes, and I see the beauty of organized, symmetrical streets; green pastures; mountains; and turquoise lakes and rivers. Everything is flowing in sync with the order and beauty of our intelligent Creator.

Above the clouds I find that the sun is still shining and I hear the Holy Spirit say: "Despite yourself—your inadequacies, failures, and frustrations—I am transforming even your darkness into My light and order. The blood of Jesus *is* sufficient for your inadequacies, and I *am* completing the good work I have begun in your life." Beloved, release your inadequacies, failures, and frustrations to Yeshua and receive Father God's view of your life today.

> *Thank You, Lord, for Yeshua's blood that was shed for me. I let go of my oppressive thoughts and concerns to trust that Your blood washes away my inadequacies and failures. I fix my eyes on You, Father, and receive Your vision of my life. I see Your light, order, and beauty, which surround me and prevail despite all my mistakes and imperfections.*

From Brokenness to Beauty

> But we have this treasure in earthen vessels, so that the surpassing greatness of the power will be of God and not from ourselves.
>
> —2 CORINTHIANS 4:7

I WANT TO ENCOURAGE you today to keep pressing in to Yeshua Jesus. You *are* making a difference!

The unseen enemy will tell you that you just keep failing, that you're insignificant, or that you aren't making any positive impact upon those around you. In fact, these kinds of thoughts enter my head when I sit down to write a word from the Lord to encourage others. As I sit at the computer, there's a war going on inside me. It begins with an anxiety that rises up within me, replaying subconscious messages that I have nothing of value to share.

If your life is like mine, you daily experience challenges that can seem insurmountable. That's because our unseen enemy seeks to intimidate us through thoughts and words so we feel defeated, retreat, and give up our good fight to carry the good news of Father's love. But beloved of God, be of good courage, and *don't give up the fight*. Rebuke the liar, for the truth is that you have been chosen; called out from a fallen, dying world; and justified in the courts of heaven as righteous, even as Jesus is righteous! You reign under the law of the Spirit of life in Christ Jesus (Rom. 8:2). The blood of Jesus actively covers every mistake, weakness, and failure so that in God's hands all brokenness is transformed into life-giving beauty.

Indeed, the "thorn" in your flesh—the insecurity Satan uses to intimidate—is what brings you to the end of yourself so that Yeshua's powerful Spirit can arise within you. Be encouraged today. Through your imperfect clay vessel, God's powerful, loving Spirit is revealing Jesus as the hope and the way.

> *Father, thank You for this earthen vessel that You created for Your glory. I let go of my attempts to be perfect and grab hold of Your strength and power. You have claimed me as Your own through the blood of Jesus, so reign now within me to bring glory to Yourself.*

DAY 3

The God of Life and Hope

For the heart of this people has become dull, with their ears they scarcely hear, and they have closed their eyes, otherwise they would see with their eyes, hear with their ears, and understand with their heart and return, and I would heal them.

—MATTHEW 13:15

WHEN HE WALKED the earth, Jesus was surrounded by a spiritually blind people who did what they had always done and thus reaped what they had always reaped. He was surrounded by an oppressed people who thoughtlessly followed the ways of their society. Most would never look up to seek the divine revelation and life Jesus came to give. May God gift us today with a hunger and thirst that drive us to look for more than what we have always received!

During our mission trips to Africa, people in very remote areas who have never heard the gospel of Jesus stop their daily activities and walk many miles to attend the crusade festivals we lead. Setting aside their comfort and normal routines, they desperately seek to find what their hearts and souls need most—the God of life and hope. Thousands of people accept Jesus as their Savior at these meetings. Many are supernaturally healed, and all are touched by the living, eternal God, who reaches down to change the lives of His people.

Like these precious souls, won't you cease your striving today? Look up and talk to your almighty Creator and Savior. Storm the gates of heaven in prayer, and ask Father to let heaven come down into your daily life. When you do this, you can expect God to respond. You can expect to hear from Him. You can expect to experience His supernatural presence and power. Through the blood of Jesus *all* things are possible.

> *Lord, may my heart never become dull. I ask You to gift me with a hunger and thirst for You that makes me seek You as a deer pants after water. Give me ears that hear, eyes that see, and a heart that chases hard after You. I look to You, Father. You alone can fill the longings of my heart. You alone can bring the change I seek. Lord, I release my striving to You. Let heaven come and invade every aspect of my day. Come and supernaturally move the mountains in my life. I put my trust in You, Father, because You have everything I need.*

Reflect His Glory

He says, "Be still, and know that I am God; I will be
exalted among the nations, I will be exalted in the earth."
—PSALM 46:10, NIV

OUR NATURAL INCLINATION is to think the world
revolves around us. Even for those of us who seek to
follow Jesus, our fears and insecurities propel us to focus
on ourselves. Oftentimes our hearts and souls need to be
put in alignment with truth from our Father so we will
grow, thrive, and fulfill the call upon our lives.

In Ezekiel 36 we find Father God correcting the souls
of His children. He says: "It is not for your sake…that I
am about to act, but for My holy name.…I will vindi-
cate the holiness of My great name.…Then the nations
will know that I am the LORD…when I prove Myself holy
among you in their sight" (vv. 22–23). What a wake-up
call! The entire purpose of God moving on our behalf is
that His holiness and glory would shine! Our lives revolve
around God, like planets around the sun, and we live to
reflect the power and greatness of God.

The Lord went on to say: "I will cleanse you from all
your filthiness and from all your idols. Moreover, I will

give you a new heart and put a new spirit within you; and I will remove the heart of stone from your flesh and give you a heart of flesh. I will put My Spirit within you and cause you to walk in My statutes, and you will be careful to observe My ordinances…so you will be My people, and I will be your God….I am not doing this for your sake….I will cause the cities to be inhabited, and the waste places will be rebuilt….Then they will know that I am the LORD" (Ezek. 36:25–38).

Beloved, by God's power we are transformed, and anything holy and good in us must be understood as coming from God and not from ourselves so the Lord receives all the glory and honor! Let's repent of our self-centered fears and insecurities and of being focused on the material world. Let us declare that the Lord reigns over our lives and all that exists. Be still and know that He is God.

It's all about You, Lord. I repent of my self-centered and world-centered thoughts and actions. Cleanse me from the idols of this world. Lord, I let go to lose myself in Your holiness, power, and greatness. I praise You for who You are, almighty God. Complete the good work You have begun in me that I may reflect Your glory!

Experience Your Eden

Then the Lord God took the man and put him into
the garden of Eden to cultivate it and keep it.

—GENESIS 2:15

THOUGH OUR WORLD has been corrupted by sin and
is filled with struggles, because you have been born
again by the Spirit of God, you can experience God's
Garden of Eden!

Yes, this garden of God's Spirit now dwells within you.
You can know the love, joy, peace, and intimacy with
Father that Adam and Eve once enjoyed, but you must
cultivate and keep it. We must cultivate relationship with
God's Spirit within in order to experience His garden of
beauty, love, and joy.

The maiden in the Song of Solomon said to her beloved,
"Come away...and be like a gazelle or like a young stag on
the spice-laden mountains" (Song of Sol. 8:14, NIV). Dear
one, by the cleansing power of Jesus' blood, let go of the
heaviness of this world and follow the Spirit of Yeshua.
Cultivate your inner Garden of Eden by talking to the
Lord about the challenges you face as you follow Him
through the highs and the lows of your life. Call upon

the Holy Spirit to uproot any inner "weeds" and replace them with His faith, love, mercy, and wisdom. Faithfully speak God's Word over yourself and your circumstances to cultivate God's beauty within and release His strength and victory. As you run into your Garden of Eden with God by communing with His Spirit, you will experience His peace, provision, and abiding joy.

> *Lord, I open my heart to You. Reveal the thorns and weeds of pain, shame, rejection, and fear that must go now through the power of Your blood and name. All challenges I face are released to You. "Though I walk through the valley of the shadow of death…You are with me," and I shall not fear (Ps. 23:4).*
>
> *Faithful, almighty Father, take the wheel, for You are my Shepherd, and You keep me on the right path. I follow You with all my heart, mind, and strength (Matt. 22:37). Close every door that leads to destruction, and open every door that leads to Your goodness (Matt. 7:13–14). As we journey up the mountains together, I am transformed into Your image with ever-increasing glory (2 Cor. 3:18, NIV). May I never neglect Your garden, and daily cultivate it to experience the beauty of intimacy with You.*

Joy and Hope in a Hopeless Land

> We know that we are of God, and that the whole world
> lies in the power of the evil one. And we know that the
> Son of God has come, and has given us understanding
> so that we may know Him who is true; and we are in Him
> who is true, in His Son Jesus Christ....Little children,
> guard yourselves from idols.
>
> —1 JOHN 5:19–21

WE LIVE IN the world where Satan resides. His spirit of darkness acts like a strong gravitational force that seeks to pull us away from God and onto a downward path of destruction and death. Our enemy is in competition with God for our attention. His goal is for us to be like him and live selfishly, apart from God, and destined for eternal destruction.

In Jeremiah 2:13, God says: "For My people have committed two evils: They have forsaken Me, the fountain of living waters, to hew for themselves cisterns, broken cisterns that can hold no water." Our Father is jealous for our attention. He knows that when we identify ourselves through what we own or what others say or think, we'll be tragically disappointed. Material things, prestigious careers, and others' affirmation never satisfy the longings of our hearts. Father alone holds the key to His child's identity. When you look to Him, "the LORD will guide you always; he will satisfy your needs in a sun-scorched land and will strengthen your frame. You will be like a well-watered garden, like a spring whose waters never fail" (Isa. 58:11, NIV).

Beloved, be vigilant to cling to and find life in Father God, His love, and His eternal kingdom. Jesus prayed, "Now this is eternal life: that they know you, the only true God, and Jesus Christ, whom you have sent" (John 17:3). I challenge you to look upward and reset your thinking today by reading and asking the Holy Spirit for revelation of Ephesians 1. Align your heart and mind according to these truths that reveal who you are in Messiah: redeemed, forgiven, chosen, the recipient of a great inheritance, and so much more. Knowing yourself in your Savior girds you with everlasting joy!

> *Father, You alone can truly satisfy the longings of my heart. Set my mind and heart on You. Like a horse with blinders on, fix my eyes on You so I don't turn to the right or left but remain steadfast with my gaze set on You, my goal and prize. Reveal Yourself to me through the words of Ephesians 1, and strengthen me as I discover my identity in You.*

Begin With the End in Mind

I am the Alpha and the Omega, the first and the last, the beginning and the end.

—Revelation 22:13

"Yes, ma'am. I will get those oxygen tanks out to your dad's apartment tomorrow morning." The serviceman promised to deliver the portable oxygen tanks for my elderly father on Saturday morning, but Saturday came and went, and the serviceman never arrived.

Day in and day out, we're faced with broken promises, broken people, and a broken world. Again and again, our needs and expectations fail to be met. The frustration this triggers can easily cause us to tumble into sin and stress, which harms our intricate, sensitive human vessels. But in the heat of our emotions, the still, small voice of God is beckoning us to push the reset button in our brains.

Beloved, heed and respond to God's still, small voice within today. Stepping back from broken situations to get His viewpoint equips us to rule our spirits. Focusing on the small details of our daily lives frustrates us and causes us to sin. Father wants us to see from His broader view. When we get His perspective, we no longer see the frustrating details that were causing us to lose our way.

We trust that the Lord sees both the beginning and the end and knows how to steer us safely to His desired destination.

When the serviceman never arrived with the oxygen tanks for my dad, I heeded the Lord's still, small voice and stepped back to see from God's perspective. I saw that I am in the end times, where brokenness prevails, and I remembered Father's faithfulness in the past. I knew He would work all things in my life together for good, and I laughed at the enemy, knowing he would not prevail in my life. Trusting in Father's care, I had mercy on the imperfect people involved in the medical system and looked to the Lord for His way through the complications keeping me from my goal. As I responded to Father's still, small voice, peace and joy replaced my frustration and anger.

Today you'll face challenging situations that will test you. But heeding that small inner voice to step back and see from the view of our Alpha and Omega will transform your thoughts, emotions, and responses so you will end up at His desired destination.

> *Thank You for Your voice that breaks into my world today, Lord. You know the end from the beginning. Release Your heart and vision into me. Equip me to recalculate my steps in accordance with Your will. Steer me safely to my destination in You.*

Be of Good Cheer

Create in me a clean heart, O God, and renew a stead-fast spirit within me....Restore to me the joy of Your salvation and sustain me with a willing spirit.

—PSALM 51:10, 12

BELOVED, BE OF good cheer: though sin separates us from God (Isa. 59:2), Yeshua has gone before us to pave the way for us to experience our Father's love and truth. Accepting that Yeshua's death on the cross paid the penalty for our sin is often seen as a onetime experience. But the key to moving into greater depths of the joy-filled, love relationship our Father desires to have with us is to discover a lifestyle of repentance.

The works of the flesh (sin) create a barrier that keeps us from experiencing the love and presence of Father God. The priests who served in the Old Testament temple knew well that the presence of our holy God would not manifest until the issue of sin was addressed at the altar of sacrifice. To experience the Holy Spirit in our mortal temples, we must apply this principle. As we humbly fall to our knees each day, repenting of the thoughts and actions we engage in without regard for our Creator, we'll experience

Yeshua's blood washing away all that has kept us from truly knowing Father's love and forgiveness.

Whenever we feel a heavy oppression upon us, the way out of this torment and into Father's peaceful, loving presence is to acknowledge the darkness and plead the blood of Jesus over our souls to receive a revelation of Father's forgiveness, love, and truth. Father desires to replace the sin, darkness, and oppression that plague our hearts with His healing love and presence.

To truly seal your heart with Father's joy and good cheer, look up and overwhelm Satan's lies by proclaiming God's Word. Proclaim who you are in Messiah. (Use, for example, Romans 8 to declare that you are rescued from darkness, your flesh is crucified with Jesus, and you live according to the law of the Spirit of life.) Proclaim who God is to you, and thank Him for what He has done.

The Lord is truly our Shepherd and compass. Let's lead a lifestyle of repentance, continually applying Yeshua's blood over our hearts so we encounter and are transformed by Father's love and truth.

> *Thank You, Yeshua, for Your blood that covers my sin and releases me into the presence of my loving Father. Continue to wash me and transform me so that I may experience my Comforter, the Holy Spirit, and walk with my Father in joy and good cheer.*

Withdraw to Spend Time With Jesus

But Jesus often withdrew to lonely places and prayed.
—LUKE 5:16, NIV

HOW OFTEN DO you steal away from work, family, and friends to spend time with the Lord? Jesus *often* withdrew to talk with His Father, and He is the perfect Son of God. How much more do we need to withdraw to an alone place to spend time talking with God?

If Yeshua, our mentor and teacher, often withdrew to be alone with Father God, then doing so must be a key to living a supernatural life. Jesus was God incarnate and had all power, yet He still made it a priority to spend time communing with His Father. He sought Father for wisdom and strength. He sought Him to process His emotions, including His anguish over the pain He would endure on the cross. The times Yeshua spent in prayer kept Him unified with His Father and fueled Him with a heavenly power that manifested while He walked the earth.

Jesus told His disciples He could do nothing of Himself but only what He saw the Father doing (John 5:19). The same is true of us. Without Him we can do nothing. The more time we spend with Father, the more we'll know Him and experience His love, peace, joy, and wisdom.

Beloved, Jesus is calling, "Come, follow Me." He calls us to follow His pattern of frequently withdrawing to talk with Father God. Supernatural peace, satisfaction, and joy come when we steal away to talk with God. Right now take this moment to identify a place and time you can get away to talk to your Father. Write it down and remind yourself of the appointment. When the time comes for you to steal away, rebuke every hindrance Satan puts up to keep you from meeting with your first love. "Draw near to God and He will draw near to you" (Jas. 4:8).

Cherished one, as you pursue your Creator, you will discover a divine love exchange that will fuel your supernatural path through the rugged roads of this earthly life.

Father, Jesus said without You, He could do nothing. How much more is this true of me? I choose to follow Yeshua's example. I rebuke Satan's attempts to keep me from meeting with You. Father, daily I lay down my busyness and make spending time with You my priority so I can share my heart with You and listen for Your voice. Bring me into deep waters of intimacy, and wash me in Your love. May Your shalom, wisdom, and revelation be my portion each day.

Taste and See That the Lord Is Good!

O taste and see that the Lord is good; how blessed is the
man who takes refuge in Him!

—PSALM 34:8

HAVE YOU TASTED and seen that the Lord is good? Have you walked with Jesus and experienced the depth and breadth of His profound love? Yeshua entreats you to open your spiritual senses today so that you can "taste" and "see" Him and His goodness.

As Yeshua is the great treasure to be sought, the affections that tie us to this temporal world must be forsaken so we can enter into a new realm of encountering Father's Spirit. What thoughts and desires are keeping you from experiencing God's goodness? When we abandon those old thoughts and behaviors and humbly receive Yeshua's new life through repentance, our Savior opens the door for us to experience His profound love in new ways.

We cannot remain in the same default mode and expect to get different results. So what one small change will you make today to think and act differently? What step toward God and away from your default mode will you take? Perhaps you will choose to start your day by taking

Communion. Or perhaps you will just sit before the Lord, reading His Word and listening to worship music to open a door for His Spirit to flow into your heart and mind.

Are there relationships that consume your thoughts and keep you from staying centered on and experiencing our Savior's love? Most often we are distracted by fears that fill our hearts and cause us to think in ways that keep us from loving the Lord first. Let the Spirit reveal the thoughts that hold your heart in bondage and prevent you from knowing Yeshua as your first love. Let go of self-centered efforts to control your life, and find refuge in the One who is good.

It's a new day. What one thought will you rebuke in the name of Jesus and turn away from today? What one new behavior will you initiate that aligns your heart and mind with Father's heart of goodness and love? Beloved, cease doing what you've always done so you can receive something far greater than what you've experienced in the past. The Bridegroom is wooing you to follow Him to new heights and depths in Him.

> *Come, Holy Spirit. Fill my mind with Your thoughts. I turn away from the thoughts that attach me to this world, and I receive Your heart, mind, and will today. Equip me to keep moving toward You step-by-step, that I may taste and see You, O lover of my soul.*

Your Story—Written by the Hand of God

Your eyes saw my unformed body; all the days ordained
for me were written in your book before one of them
came to be.

—Psalm 139:16, NIV

A S A CHILD I developed a strong faith in my loving
Lord Jesus. But at the age of eighteen this faith was
shaken. While attending college, I encountered students
from a multitude of religious backgrounds, which caused
me to wonder whether I had merely been brainwashed by
my family and church to believe in Jesus. I hungered to
know the truth, and I avidly searched for it by attending
philosophy classes and Bible studies, asking others about
their beliefs, and crying out to the Lord at night.

I prayed for five years, telling God that unless He
revealed Himself to me as Lord I could no longer believe
in Him. I also asked Him to send me a man from Himself
to be my husband if He truly was Lord. Throughout
those five years, I felt my prayer was not being answered,
and my once strong faith in God began to erode. Soon
I decided that life was merely about pursuing pleasure,
and I directed all my efforts toward this self-centered

goal. Eventually my amoral life spiraled into a dark and depraved state, and I lacked inner peace.

At the lowest point of my life, I encountered a Jewish neighbor, whom I knew from high school. He told me about a vision he'd had of Jesus that revealed to him that Yeshua is Lord. As he spoke, I felt a surreal sensation, which I later came to know was the Spirit of God touching me. Then I heard a simple statement, "I am the way, the truth, and the life" (John 14:6), which answered my five years of prayer. That Jewish neighbor soon became my husband and the answer to the second part of my prayer! Together we are now Jew and Gentile, one in Messiah, building God's kingdom and preparing for His return!

Beloved, your story, like mine, has many chapters, and the finger of God has written it. Father has a plan, a purpose, and a destiny for you that He completes as you partner with Him. Be not dismayed by your questions and the prayers that are not yet answered. It may take years for revelation and fulfillment to come, but *it will come*. Keep seeking, knocking, asking questions, and following His still, small voice to discover your identity and complete your destiny.

> *Lord, I wait upon You for Your answers. I keep pressing onward and upward in You. By Your mighty hand, complete the good work You have begun in me.*

DAY 12

Commune With the One Who Is Trustworthy

Come to Me, all who are weary and heavy-laden, and
I will give you rest. Take My yoke upon you and learn
from Me, for I am gentle and humble in heart, and you
will find rest for your souls. For My yoke is easy and My
burden is light.

—MATTHEW 11:28–30

WE ALL HAVE hidden thoughts and secret burdens
that we carry. This may be due to fears of being
rejected or possibly because these thoughts, burdens, or
memories are like delicate, treasured pearls that we want
to protect from those who would not know how to handle
them.

But beloved, there is One who *can* be trusted with your
"pearls." In fact, He already knows the intimate details of
your life. He understands you fully and loves you *unconditionally*. Won't you open your heart to this trustworthy
friend?

The One to trust says, "Look into My eyes and come to
Me." He says, "Come to Me, and I will come to you. Bring
all your thoughts and memories. Bring your sin, failures,
and mistakes. Give Me your darkened heart and mind.

Bring all the shame and the generations of lies and deceptions that you bear."

The One to trust says: "I see all your hidden thoughts and the tears you shed. Look up to find Me. I know you intimately. Set the eyes of your heart upon Me, and bring all your baggage to Me. I have poured out My blood, removing your sin. My living water washes you clean, and I transform your ashes into beauty. I take your troubled thoughts and sin into Myself, and in the fire of My love all darkness is destroyed. Come to Me with all that you are, for I am your Shepherd, who keeps you safe and carries you to the Father to receive His outpouring of love and your inheritance of glory!"

Beloved, it's time to stop keeping secrets within your heart. Lay them bare before your Father, who loves you like no other. Talk to Him about the intimate secrets and pain hidden in your heart. Abraham believed and trusted God, and it was reckoned to him as righteousness, and he was called the friend of God (Jas. 2:23). Today, experience the Lord as your deepest, closest friend by opening your heart and trusting Him with your deepest secrets.

I open my heart today, Lord, to share with You my deepest secrets, the things I have never talked about with anyone else. I trust You as my best friend, who loves me and cares deeply for me.

DAY 13

The Key to Your Shalom

Be anxious for nothing, but in everything by prayer and supplication with thanksgiving let your requests be made known to God. And the peace of God, which surpasses all comprehension, will guard your hearts and your minds in Christ Jesus.

—PHILIPPIANS 4:6–7

AS WE HEAD into more end-time headwinds, none of us can escape the negativity that seeks to entangle us. Thoughts and proclamations of doom and destruction threaten to defeat us. Fear grips each of us every day, but this fear is not of the Lord. In Him we should experience only a freeing, righteous fear of God. But how can we overcome fear when we are continually faced with threats of illness, death, and loss of relationships with family, friends, and coworkers? The Lord says we do this through thanksgiving!

It may seem like a crazy idea when we're facing threats to our well-being on every side. But I challenge you to retrain your brain to look for all the signs of the positive, life-giving hand of God at work in your life. It does not matter what your circumstance is; the beautiful, life-giving God of creation is surrounding you every moment.

Look for His handiwork, listen for His voice, and thank Him for what He is doing. As we look to see the face of God and His goodness all around us, we will discover endless blessings. What's more, our lives will supernaturally move toward hope, newness of life, and joy.

The Bible says, "Finally, brethren, whatever is true, whatever is honorable, whatever is right, whatever is pure, whatever is lovely, whatever is of good repute, if there is any excellence and if anything worthy of praise, dwell on these things" (Phil. 4:8). Thinking and speaking true, life-giving words about ourselves and others has power to change a negative circumstance into something positive. So, beloved one, be intentional about speaking words of thanksgiving, and watch your world supernaturally transform from fear into shalom, the peace that surpasses all understanding.

Thank You, Lord, that I am alive to complete Your plan for my life. Thank You, Father, for sending Jesus and Your Holy Spirit so I know I am not alone and am equipped for any battle. Thank You for the warming sun and the cleansing rains. And thank You, Lord, for giving me eyes to see in the Spirit, which equips me to focus on the beauty, life, and hope that surround me.

DAY 14

A Divine Exchange of Poured-Out Love

Therefore, I will allot Him a portion with the great, and He will divide the booty with the strong; because He poured out Himself to death, and was numbered with the transgressors; yet He Himself bore the sin of many, and interceded for the transgressors.

—Isaiah 53:12

God's Word encourages us to "run with endurance the race that is set before us" (Heb. 12:1), but doing so can leave us feeling weary and depleted. Once during a time of complete exasperation I threw my arms up angrily at God and cried out, "What do You want from me? What more?" Immediately, His crushing response came: "All of you. I gave you all of Me, so you must give Me *all* of you."

His weighty presence and penetrating words instantly settled the matter and brought me into a new place of peace and strength. He spoke to me of the deep, dynamic relationship I have with Him. In this covenantal relationship I am an active participant in a passionate, divine exchange. I must pour my life out for God so that He can fill me up with Himself; then in turn I am to again empty myself out. This poured-out love exchange continues on and on and on, seemingly without end. Supernaturally, through this process I find myself changing and being transformed from the inside out!

We can know how to live this poured-out life by looking to Yeshua's example. Jesus went before us so we could model what He did. Scripture says He "emptied Himself" and became "obedient to the point of death, even death on a cross. For this reason also, God highly exalted Him, and bestowed on Him the name which is above every name" (Phil. 2:7–9). Unto the Father and for our justification, Jesus allowed Himself to be poured out. Because of His sacrificial love, our victory over every battle is sealed and we have God's Spirit living within us to equip us in overcoming every obstacle.

Beloved, you are in an amazing, intimate love exchange with the Lord. Keep going to your Source, giving Him *all* of yourself so He can fill you up. Keep taking from His life-giving Spirit, and keep pouring it back out!

> *Lord, thank You for pouring Yourself out in love to give me new life, hope, and strength. With my eyes of love upon You, I give You all of me. I come to You empty, asking You to fill me afresh with Your Spirit, Your power, Your love, and Your Word. Fill me to overflowing so I can then pour into others.*

Bless the Lord, Adon Olam, and Bless Yourself

> Blessed be the God and Father of our Lord Jesus Christ, who has blessed us with every spiritual blessing in the heavenly places in Christ.
>
> —EPHESIANS 1:3

BELOVED, DON'T LET the enemy torment you with negative thoughts and vain imaginations about the future. Rebuke his lies and word curses off your life. You were created in love to shine, so arise now to *bless* your life with thoughts and words that oppose the enemy's negative reports, accusations, and prophecies of doom.

Satan will incessantly fill our minds with his bad reports about our circumstances and the unknown details of our future. But God knows all the details of our lives—past, present, and future—for He is Adon Olam, Master of the universe. He is the One with the master plan for our lives, and He will be sure to complete His good work in us. Although it can be uncomfortable when He stretches us to conform us to His glorious image, He provides everything we need to become more like Him, mending our broken lives and giving us joy in Him.

Your loving Father will *never* leave you or forsake you, and He is faithful to carry the load you bear, but *you must release it to Him.* Give Him your load today. Release all the negative thoughts, shameful deeds, and inner oppressions to Jesus. Rebuke all the tormenting lies, destructive thoughts, and word curses through the blood of Jesus.

Bless yourself—bless your body, your situation, your endeavors, your loved ones—and pray for those who oppose you. Retrain your brain with positive thoughts and confessions that express trust in the plan Adon Olam has for your life. Thoughts and spoken words hold power in the spiritual realm, and they have authority over the physical realm. So begin thinking and speaking *blessing* over every part of your precious life. Practice putting ill thoughts about yourself or others under the blood of Jesus, and speak forgiveness and love over yourself and others. In doing so, you will transform your world to experience healing and spiritual blessings beyond measure.

> *Forgive me, Lord, for agreeing with the enemy's accusations and negative reports. I rebuke every lie and word curse spoken against me, for the law of the Spirit of life in Messiah Jesus has set me free from the law of sin and death (Rom. 8:2). I bless You, Lord, and the life You have given me. My hope and trust are in You, Your provision, and Your good plans for my life.*

DAY 16

Appendage of God

Do you not know that your bodies are members of Christ?
Shall I then take away the members of Christ and make
them members of a prostitute? May it never be!
—1 Corinthians 6:15

In the intense times we live in, with people busily
running to and fro, trying to keep up with the stressful
demands brought on by their jobs and technology, I pray
often for Jesus to equip His body to keep Him at the front
and center of our lives. Setting aside the first portion of
the day to spend with our Father shows that He is our
first love, and this is a time He uses to reset our hearts to
be in tune with His.

During my "set apart" times, I seek to lay all my weaknesses, failures, and cares at the feet of Jesus to enter into
an intimate time of connection with my almighty Father.
One morning, after releasing my cares to Yeshua, I began
calling on the Holy Spirit for revelation regarding today's
verse. The Spirit of God moved upon me and deeply con-
nected me with Yeshua through a profound vision.

The Spirit began by first showing me that the word
member refers to a limb or appendage, as in an arm or
leg, and that as believers in Messiah Jesus we are integral

parts of Him. As the Spirit revealed this truth to me, I suddenly saw, through the eyes of my heart, the Lord in bodily form extending Himself and His hand to me. My body became the finger that stretched forth from His hand pointing toward the earth. His loving, almighty being filled me profoundly, releasing new revelation and understanding about situations I was facing.

Paul wrote, "For the body is not one member, but many. If the foot says, 'Because I am not a hand, I am not a part of the body,' it is not for this reason any the less a part of the body. And if the ear says, 'Because I am not an eye, I am not a part of the body,' it is not for this reason any the less a part of the body....God has placed the members, each one of them, in the body, just as He desired" (1 Cor. 12:14–16, 18).

Beloved, when you received Yeshua as your Savior, you became part of His spiritual body, the church. Now you are His appendage, releasing divine love to a world in need of a Savior.

> *Here I am, Lord, an appendage of Your body extended into this earthly realm for Your glory. Release Your unconditional love through me into every situation that I face today.*

Chosen to Follow

You did not choose Me but I chose you, and appointed you that you would go and bear fruit, and that your fruit would remain, so that whatever you ask of the Father in My name He may give to you.

—John 15:16

Though I may at times become frustrated or hurt by those who boldly walk in self-righteousness, bitterness, anger, unforgiveness, or unbelief, the truth is that without God's sovereign grace upon my life, my heart and actions would be no different from theirs. The Lord tells us that apart from Him our works are but filthy rags (Isa. 64:6) and that faith itself is a gift (Eph. 2:8–9).

In truth, we have faith in the Lord simply because He chose to impart His Spirit of revelation to us. I did not choose my parents or the circumstances that I grew up under. God chose these for me, and He has lovingly intervened throughout my life to reveal Himself to me. He does the same for each of us.

In His love for us, God sovereignly chose us for Himself, even as He chose the Jewish people as a nation for Himself (Deut. 7:6; John 15:16). But He also calls us to *release* our fleshly will to embrace His will. He calls us to respond to His love by letting go of our worldly affections, abandoning our old ways to find ourselves in Him. He calls us to come into divine alignment with the Father, Son, and Holy Spirit. Father's Spirit woos and whispers to us to follow Him wherever He leads.

During a time when my husband was crying out in emotional pain to the Lord, the Holy Spirit said to him, "If you would cooperate, it wouldn't hurt so much." Father has gifted us with the revelation of Himself, yet we must strive to stick close to Him, just as children cling to their parents for safety and to keep from getting lost. Today, endeavor to enter through Yeshua's narrow gate (Matt. 7:13–14) by letting go of old impulses and desires and choosing to cherish and follow your beloved Savior. As you do, the peaceful fruit of righteousness (Heb. 12:11) and joy will fill your life!

> *Thank You, Lord, for choosing me in love for Yourself! Humbled and grateful, I respond by letting go of my life and coming into agreement with Your will for me. Make me sensitive to Your leading so I don't miss Your promptings. I want to follow You so my life will bring forth the peaceful fruit of righteousness. I choose to honor, love, and cherish You and to follow wherever You lead me.*

DAY 18

Unity in Messiah Jesus

If two of you agree on earth about anything that they may ask, it shall be done for them by My Father who is in heaven. For where two or three have gathered together in My name, I am there in their midst.

—MATTHEW 18:19–20

IMAGINE FOR A moment the living, moving Spirit of God dwelling within your sisters and brothers in Messiah. Now envision each one carrying this Spirit into a prayer meeting. With each additional person, the presence of God increases in the room, and His diverse personality begins to manifest as the saints interact.

This is what happens when the body of Yeshua dwells together in unity. "It is like the precious oil upon the head, coming down upon the beard, even Aaron's beard, coming down upon the edge of his robes" (Ps. 133:2). The oil that flowed down Aaron's beard represents the anointing. There is an anointing that flows out of unity within the body of Messiah.

Father God longs for His children to humbly lay down every prideful grudge at the foot of the cross and come together in His Spirit so that mountains are moved and the enemy is overcome. The Scriptures say, "If one can overpower him who is alone, two can resist him. A cord of three strands is not quickly torn apart" (Eccles. 4:12).

Beloved, there is power in numbers. As we join together to take the gospel to the world, the life-changing power of God is released upon the earth. So by the blood and name of Yeshua, overcome those voices that tell you not to financially and prayerfully support organizations that minister the gospel of Jesus. Meet with sisters and brothers in Messiah, in whatever format is possible, so the Spirit of God is stirred up and prayers against the enemy are answered.

In opposition to Satan, let's boldly band together so that we are strengthened and Father's truth and love are spread to the ends of the earth. As the gospel of the kingdom is "preached in the whole world as a testimony to all the nations," then comes the return of our Lord and Savior (Matt. 24:14)! *United in Messiah, we gain strength for today and make an impact for tomorrow.*

> *Father, forgive me for holding on to hurts and offenses because of pride. I humbly choose to let go of the grudges and offenses that have held me in bondage and rendered me weak and powerless. I band together with Your church, which is naturally imperfect but perfected in You. Fill us and equip us to move mountains and build Your kingdom!*

DAY 19

See Yourself in Spirit and in Truth

And we know that God causes all things to work together
for good to those who love God, to those who are called
according to His purpose. For those whom He foreknew,
He also predestined to become conformed to the image
of His Son.

—ROMANS 8:28–29

You HAVE A destiny in God that no perceived weakness
or flaw can thwart. The Lord our Creator has written
your story (Ps. 139:16). Being saved by the blood of Jesus
means that your name is written in the Lamb's Book of
Life (Rev. 21:27). Beloved of God, your story has already
been written in God's heart (Jer. 29:11). With Father at the
wheel, His Spirit will drive you, albeit on a bumpy road,
to your final destination of eternal life with Yeshua.

Your artistic Creator made you with a unique character
and personality, and strengths and weaknesses. As you
continually surrender yourself to Him, the Spirit of God
imparts gifts, knowledge, wisdom, revelation, and pas-
sions that equip you to complete your assignment in life.
You can depend on Yeshua to transform even your weaknesses into strengths that bring glory to God!

This same pattern of transformation occurs as we

release people and situations to God. There will always be individuals and circumstances that upset us. The source of our frustration may even be ourselves! These are the times to find refuge in the Lord's unconditional love and grace. Thank Him for His love and sovereignty over your life. Trusting in your Father, release to Jesus the people and situations that grieve you. Let God's merciful Spirit conform you into the image of His perfect Son.

Our Maker and Redeemer sees great beauty in you and takes delight in perfecting you. So be at peace with who you are. *Be nothing more and nothing less than who God created you to be.* Yeshua knows the pain and struggles on the rugged road you travel; He is your constant companion. Though a flawed work in process, you will make it to the end as you walk with the One who sees you as beautiful and already made perfect!

> *Father, so often I see only weaknesses, flaws, mistakes, and failures. Forgive me. I receive Your grace to see myself as You do, already perfected through the blood of Jesus. Thank You for making me special and unique. My weaknesses will not hinder me. I will fulfill Your plans for my life through the gifts You have imparted to me. Holy Spirit, complete the work You have begun in me, using every situation I face in life to make me more like Jesus.*

DAY 20

No More Business as Usual

And He has said to me, "My grace is sufficient for you, for power is perfected in weakness." Most gladly, therefore, I will rather boast about my weaknesses, so that the power of Christ may dwell in me.

—2 CORINTHIANS 12:9

JUST BEFORE THE COVID-19 pandemic, the Holy Spirit apprehended me with the words "no more business as usual." I knew that with those words the Lord was summoning His people to release some of our old, good ways of operating in order to move upward to new, better ways of functioning. His words issued a mandate for us to not look back but look forward and follow Him wherever He leads.

The Lord's words sobered me. We are in new times, and with new times come new trials and difficulties to overcome. As I continued to seek Father for revelation of His words, I sensed that as we near Yeshua's return the obstacles and challenges we face are becoming so overwhelming that the only way to overcome them is by seeking and following Him at all costs. Take no comfort in the strength of the flesh, for God's way of victory will come only when you lay yourself bare before Him. Hold nothing back from Him. All that is important must be surrendered to Him in faith.

At times, we will feel this is impossible to do. But in utter humility, we must relinquish everything and trust the One who reigns above all. When nothing seems to make sense and everything seems to be a mess, put your heart into the hands of the Father and His sacrificed Son. This is circumcision of the heart.

Beloved, it is a new season with new problems, trials, and tribulations. The old default ways of getting by will no longer support you. But be of good cheer. Yeshua's love and supernatural ways not only will get you through your trials but will cause you to soar like the eagles above every challenge you face. Let go of what has kept you stuck in the past, and persevere in Yeshua. Remember, Jesus secured your victory through His death and resurrection, so your job now is to cling to Him!

> *Father, I choose to follow where You lead. I release the old ways and provisions to embrace Your new strategies and the gifts You are releasing to me. Lord, I surrender and hold nothing back from You. Strengthen me by Your Spirit to overcome the new obstacles and challenges that come my way. Thank You for the victory You have secured for me in Yeshua!*

Don't Stop

Pursue righteousness, godliness, faith, love, perseverance and gentleness. Fight the good fight of faith; take
hold of the eternal life to which you were called.

—1 TIMOTHY 6:11–12

HAVE YOU EVER felt as if you were spinning your
wheels, striving to live and move in the Lord, yet
finding you were doing the same things and getting the
same results? Have you ever felt that no matter how hard
you worked, you were never good enough? The Lord says:

Don't stop persevering to seek Me and follow Me.
You *are* making a difference. I created you, and
your life matters. You *are* loved and valued—by
Me and by others you touch each day.

Life and relationships—that's what's happening
in your day. Every prayer, every smile, every hug,
and every word of encouragement, wisdom, and
revelation is imparting My eternal life into a dying
world. I am completing the good work that I began
in you. The gates of hell cannot prevail against you,
and I *will* complete My plan for your life.

Keep seeking My face, My presence, and My
Word. Keep following Me as best you know how,

trusting and confident that I am involved in every detail of your life. Know that My rod and staff *will* keep you on the path of righteousness.

Precious one, giving up always leads to greater problems, but leaning in to Yeshua, the victor, opens up new hope and in time secures your triumph over every obstacle. Remember, you *are* making a difference because Jesus is *in* you. Beloved, "the mystery which has been hidden from the past ages and generations, but has now been manifested to His saints…is Christ in you, the hope of glory" (Col. 1:26–27). Father's transforming love, peace, grace, forgiveness, and joy are increasing within you as you keep contending to die to your old self to receive more of His Spirit and take on more of His character.

Through your life, God's love, goodness, and strength are manifest on the earth. So no matter what challenges you face, *keep pressing in to Jesus. Don't stop!*

Father, I release my weakness to You so that Your strength is perfected in me. Your Word says that in due season I will reap if I faint not. I trust You, and I receive Your grace to keep seeking You, persevering in prayer, and encouraging others. Thank You, Yeshua, for Your victorious Spirit that lives inside of me. You are my living hope for every situation.

A Matter of the Heart

Trust in the Lord with all your heart and do not lean on
your own understanding.

—PROVERBS 3:5

WHILE MANY PEOPLE struggle with compulsively
looking at their cell phones for entertainment and
the latest social media posts, I have never thought of
myself as addicted to my phone. My husband would often
warn me not to look at my phone all the time, but I would
tell him that I only use it in a utilitarian manner, to be
there for family and ministerial needs.

Just before I departed on a trip to Israel, a clear image
of my very old cell phone suddenly ceasing to function
flashed into my mind. Of course, I immediately prayed
against that, as all my notes for managing the logistics of
ministering, filming, touring, prayer, and study in Israel
were in my phone. But sure enough, just hours after we
arrived in Israel, that is exactly what happened.

Jet-lagged and stressed from travel, I began to panic.
While my husband slept, I paced the floor petitioning the
Lord to touch my phone and make it work again. When
He did not answer, I cried out in desperation like David

did in the psalms, saying, "Lord, where are You?" Like a bolt of lightning, the Holy Spirit came upon me, revealing my heart: I *was* addicted to my phone. I was trusting in my phone to help me navigate the increasingly complicated routines of life more than I was trusting in the Lord.

In that moment, the Holy Spirit spoke to me: "Do you want to lean in to the unreliable worldly means, or do you want to lean in to Me as the source of all that you need? Do you want to walk in the natural or in the supernatural?" With my heart laid bare before the Lord, I let go, releasing all my fallible plans and resources to Him. I responded, "Lord, I want to trust in You and operate by Your supernatural means." Immediately, the peace of God that surpasses all understanding flooded my mind, body, and soul.

When I looked down, my phone suddenly lit up! With my heart peacefully resting in Father's control, I had a perfectly functioning phone throughout our time in Israel. Beloved, let the Holy Spirit reveal what your heart is trusting in for security. Let go and entrust yourself to Abba Father, leaning not on your own understanding. Discover Yeshua's peace and freedom!

> *Lord, I want to experience the adventure of Your supernatural life. I release all my fallible plans and resources to You. I let go. I trust and depend completely upon You!*

The Anointing Brings Freedom

So it will be in that day, that his burden will be removed from your shoulders and his yoke from your neck, and the yoke will be broken because of fatness.

—Isaiah 10:27

GOD GAVE MY husband and me a passion to extend our outreach beyond the United States in 2013. When we were invited to preach the gospel in Haiti, I learned that the United States and other countries were pouring millions of dollars into Haiti to lift the nation out of extreme poverty. But I was devastated to see that the many dollars spent had not relieved Haiti of the oppressive poverty.

As I spoke with missionaries who had served in Haiti for many years, I realized that years of dependence on foreign assistance and a spiritual history in which occult leaders made allegiances with demonic spirits had left many Haitians trapped in a horrible cycle of oppression. The term *zombie* has roots in voodoo, which is practiced in Haiti. It refers to a will-less, speechless human whose body has died but has been reanimated by a demonic spirit.

As if oppressed by a zombie spirit, many Haitians seemed to will-lessly keep doing what they'd always done and thus get the same results. For example, after receiving a water filtration system that purified their drinking water, one community failed to perform the required system maintenance and returned to drinking contaminated water. This served as a stark reminder to me that without the Lord breaking in to change our habits and ways of thinking, we cannot create and maintain new systems that will improve the quality of our lives. But the good news is that the anointing of God destroys yokes and sets people free from all kinds of bondage.

The word *fatness* in today's verse refers to the anointing. As we call on the Lord to release His anointing that gives us revelation and divine creativity, He empowers us to destroy negative patterns, even those that have afflicted our families for generations. The Spirit of the Lord anointed Jesus "to proclaim liberty to the captives and recovering of sight to the blind, to set at liberty those who are oppressed" (Luke 4:18–19, ESV). Let's walk in this same anointing to experience breakthrough and see others set free.

> *Father, You know the strongholds, even those from generations past, that hinder my ability to see, think, and walk in Your divine, creative, life-giving ways. Your Word says Yeshua came to set me free. I receive Yeshua's anointing, which breaks off evil yokes. Move through me by the power of Your Spirit.*

The Father's Passionate Love

Pray, then, in this way: "Our Father who is in heaven, hallowed be Your name."

—Matthew 6:9

WE ADDRESS GOD as our Father, but do we truly know Him as Father? Knowing God as Father involves an intimate relationship of childlike love and trust. So on a scale of one to ten, how well do you know God as Father?

Recently the Holy Spirit revealed to me that images of my imperfect earthly father were keeping me from truly knowing my heavenly Father. He penetrated my heart with these words:

> I embody the extremes of all human emotions, not like your father. I embody
>
> - passionate, pure love, not like your father.
> - passionate compassion, not like your father.
> - passionate mercy, not like your father.
> - passionate joy, not like your father.
> - passionate humor, not like your father.

- passionate, deep empathy, not like your father.

- passionate jealousy for you and everyone I love, not like your father.

- passionate anger and fury against evil and our enemies, not like your father.

- passionate demonstration of righteous power and authority over all, not like your father.

- passionate forgiveness, not like your father.

I am the sacrificial, passionate lover of your soul, not like your father or any other person. I am your Father, and you are Mine.

Dear child of God, you now have a trustworthy, almighty Father, who calls you to experience the heights and depths of passionate relationship with Him. I encourage you to let go of negative images of your imperfect, earthly father to embrace your loving, eternal Father. Ask Him to show you the truth of who He is, and brace yourself for an adventure in love!

O Lord, may Your passionate love and righteousness fill and overwhelm me. May I love what You love and hate what You hate. Father, I love (passionately) because You first loved me (1 John 4:19).

Choose Life

Whether, then, you eat or drink or whatever you do, do all to the glory of God.

—1 CORINTHIANS 10:31

THE OLDER WE get, the more acutely aware my husband and I become of how our choices today impact our experiences tomorrow. Choosing to repeatedly sit out in the sun to develop a "beautiful" tan can later result in wrinkled skin and even skin cancer. Choosing to eat an unbalanced diet filled with sugar, salt, and unhealthy fat can lead to cardiovascular disease, diabetes, and obesity. Choosing to marry an unbeliever can result in heartache. And choosing to mindlessly follow the crowd can result in destruction.

The enemy wants to steal our future, kill our potential, and destroy our health. But Yeshua came that we may "have life, and have it abundantly" (John 10:10). The key is that we must choose to follow God's ways to experience the life and peace He desires for us. The Lord says, "I have set before you life and death, the blessing and the curse. So choose life in order that you may live" (Deut. 30:19).

Our Father says, "Choose Me. Choose life." What we

choose every moment matters. Our choices impact the quality of our lives and the lives of others. So beloved, be aware of your thoughts throughout the day. Continually transform them by saying out loud, "I choose life." Whether you're deciding what to eat, how to spend your time, what to say to someone, or how to spend your money, say, "I choose life." In this manner you rebuke and overcome sin and death. When it's a battle to utter and agree with these words, begin by saying, "In Jesus' name and by the power of His blood, I choose life."

The Lord is our Creator, and He knows everything about us. He wants to see us prosper in every area of our lives. Choosing to follow His ways and make Him the focus of our lives will *always* lead us to prosper and triumph in Messiah Jesus.

Father, I choose You! I choose to follow Your ways. Through the blood of Jesus You have made a way for me to love You, obey Your voice, and hold fast to Your Word. Thank You for being my loving Father, who wants the best for me—to prosper me and not to harm me. Lord, remind me to call on Your life-giving Spirit when I awake and throughout the day so that I activate my powerful ability, in Jesus' name, to speak and follow Your laws. I choose You, Lord; I choose life!

Re-parented by God

Jesus answered and said to him, "Truly, truly, I say to you, unless one is born again he cannot see the kingdom of God."

—John 3:3

JESUS USED THE term *born again* to depict the new, eternal life gained by receiving Him into our being. His blood destroys the darkness that keeps us from knowing God, and His Spirit birthed within us releases revelation to see, know, and walk with God the Father!

Precious one, being born again allows you to start your life over with a new Father to re-parent you. Although earthly fathers may carry the burden of guilt and shame, your pure, unburdened heavenly Father re-parents you with perfect, endless love, grace, peace, and compassion. No matter what your parents were like when you were growing up or what choices you made in the past, your heavenly Father wants you to see yourself through His eyes. To Him you are like a beloved newborn child (1 John 3:1), freshly cleansed by Yeshua's blood.

I challenge you today to begin a new walk with Father by envisioning yourself as an innocent newborn baby looking up to learn who you are through the eyes of your loving Father. Newborns cannot see themselves, and all they know of their identity is what they see in their parents' eyes. They have no identity outside what they see in their parents' face. Father, *El Rachum* (the God of compassionate, motherly love), lovingly woos you to look to Him in prayer to discover who you are as His child. He invites you to begin a new journey of learning who you are through His eyes and His Word.

Beloved, seek the One who loves deeply, never worries, and remains confident in the future. As a child reach up to Him and release your concerns to your almighty, safe Father. Take His hand today and let Him show you the way. Allow His Spirit to carry you into a peace that passes the understanding of this world. Remember, Your Father is all-knowing and trustworthy, but *most of all He loves you.* So cling to your Daddy and follow Him to the end!

Father, thank You for making all things new and for the opportunity to learn of and know Your perfect, rachum *love. Lord, You know me better than I know myself, and You see me as I truly am. So with my trust in You, my Father, I let go of the people and things I have clung to in the past and I look to You. Let me see myself anew through Your eyes, as Your beloved child whom You love unconditionally.*

Pray for the Peace of Jerusalem

Pray for the peace of Jerusalem: "May they prosper who love you. May peace be within your walls, and prosperity within your palaces."

—Psalm 122:6–7

TRULY BLESSED ARE we who've been grafted into Christ, the Olive Tree, receiving all the blessings of Abraham and his descendants through Jesus our Messiah (Rom. 11:17)! Yeshua's gospel came to us through the Jewish people, and our Redeemer has promised to return as the Lion of Judah to set up the New Jerusalem.

Beloved, Israel and the Jewish people remain central to our faith. The Old Testament prophet Isaiah said, "Can a nation be born in a day?" In 1948 God supernaturally answered this prophetic question by restoring the State of Israel to the Jewish people in a day. His eyes continue to be upon Israel and the Jewish people ("the apple of His eye," according to Zechariah 2:8). With Israel as host of the coming Messiah Yeshua and the New Jerusalem (Ezek. 40–48; Zech. 2:4–5; Isa. 54:11–14; Rev. 3:12, 22:1), it's clear that Israel is the focal point of a major spiritual battle between Satan and Yeshua. Because Israel has enemies on its left and right, God calls us to pray for the peace of Jerusalem (Ps. 122:6–7).

We are Yeshua's church, and our prayers for Israel and the Jewish people usher in the return of our Messiah and the establishment of the New Jerusalem. I urge you to pray for the Lord to hold back Israel's enemies until the time is right and all eyes have been opened to receive Jesus and His eternal life. Pray for God's angels to be released on behalf of Israel and the Jewish people. Call for the eyes of the Jewish people to be opened to see and embrace their Messiah, Jesus. As Jewish people recognize Yeshua as their Savior, they will cry out with the Gentiles, "Baruch haba B'Shem Adonai" (Blessed is He who comes in the name of the Lord), and our beloved Yeshua will return (Rom. 11:24; Luke 13:35)!

> *Thank You for grafting me into the Olive Tree, Lord, that I may partake of You and the bless-ings You have bestowed upon Your Jewish people! I cry out for the fulfillment of every detail of Your plan. May the eyes of Your Jewish people be opened to see and follow You, and may they join the church in crying out for Your return, King Jesus. Baruch haba B'Shem Adonai* [pronounced: Ba-rook ha-ba Ba-shem Adonai]. *Blessed are You who comes in the name of the Lord! Come, Lord Jesus!*

Don't Let Satan Steal Your Sleep

It is in vain that you rise up early and go late to rest, eating the bread of anxious toil; for he gives to his beloved sleep.

—PSALM 127:2, ESV

HAVE YOU EVER lain down to receive a well-needed time of rest and restoration but found that as you closed your eyes, your mind and spirit were not in agreement with your weary body? Though you were positioned for sleep, your mind was racing and your spirit was anxious and agitated. When I was a young adolescent, I often experienced this at night. Yet through the years, the Lord revealed that He is the answer to this and *every* problem.

If you have trouble sleeping, I encourage you to stop wrestling with your flesh and begin warring in the Spirit against the enemy that is tormenting you. Remember, we do not wrestle with flesh and blood but against evil spirits and principalities (Eph. 6:12). As a young adolescent, I began reciting the Lord's Prayer to myself when I lay down to rest. I would repeat it over and over until peace came over my body. Eventually I would fall into a deep sleep. This still helps me, but I have discovered additional methods of entering into God's rest at night.

Sometimes when I feel overwhelmed with anxiety, I simply say, "The blood of Jesus." I keep repeating these words until the darkness and anxiety dissipate. As light and hope come in, I declare God's Word over my life. Jesus' blood and Word are powerful! Trials, tribulations, and human imperfections brought to the Lord in repentance are transformed under the blood of Jesus. All guilt, shame, and condemnation are removed, and Father's love and hope release our hearts and minds into rest.

Finally, beloved, envision yourself giving the wheel of your life to God! He can be trusted to go before you and transform every situation for His glory, but you must release your challenges to the Lord. Let Him fix things His way. If Jesus slept through storms (Matt. 8:24–26), we can sleep through the storms of life too! May these principles help you bring Father's love and peace into your body and soul as you lie down to rest tonight!

Father, thank You for the gift of sleep. I call for Your angels and presence to fill my bedroom when I lie down to rest. Equip me to release my cares and worries to You through the powerful name and blood of Yeshua. As Your redeemed child, I receive Your perfect shalom beyond all circumstances, and I rest peacefully while You reign over my life.

Trapped With One Way Out

In my distress I called upon the Lord, and cried to my
God for help; He heard my voice out of His temple, and
my cry for help before Him came into His ears.

—PSALM 18:6

DURING A SPIRITUAL retreat in the mountains of
Colorado, a dear friend and I went to a remote loca-
tion in the woods to seek the Lord. Upon forging through
the woods to return home, we discovered that we were
completely lost.

As my friend walked ahead of me, seeking a path out
of the woods, I looked down to discover a very large pile
of bear dung, indicating that bear could be somewhere
close by! Unsettled by the thought of encountering a bear,
I quickly passed the dung to catch up with my friend.
Nonchalantly, I shared with her that I had just passed a
large pile of bear dung. At that very moment, I looked
around and discovered that we were surrounded by tall
trees and high, deep foliage!

With concerns that a bear was nearby with nothing but
woods around us, panic set in. My mind ran out of strate-
gies for getting home. I knew there was only one hope for
us. I looked straight up to the bright blue sky and began

crying out to Jesus for the way out! My friend joined with me. The next thing we knew, we were beyond the high trees and foliage and heading back toward home! It was as if we were supernaturally transported through the thick foliage and an internal compass were placed within us to direct us out to the main road.

Beloved, with Yeshua you have an advocate and a supernatural path out of every desperate situation. If fear and panic are setting in, look up, cry out to God, and trust the Lord for the way out! As David said in Psalm 23, even when we walk through the valley of the shadow of death, we shall fear no evil, for He is with us.

Father, thank You for always hearing my cry. Your Word says You are near to all who call upon You, and You are faithful to hear and save us. Whenever I am afraid, Lord, I will look to You. I put my trust in You. I will fear no evil because I know that You are with me.

Meditate on God's Beauty

> One thing I have asked from the Lord, that I shall seek:
> That I may dwell in the house of the Lord all the days of
> my life, to behold the beauty of the Lord and to meditate
> in His temple.
>
> —PSALM 27:4

THE PUREST FORM of beauty is found in the Lord. He is true, perfect, and righteous. In Him is beauty in motion—living, moving, active beauty that is undefiled by the twisted darkness of this world. I love to just sit before Him and pray: "Open my eyes, O Lord, to see the pure essence of Your creation. Allow me to perceive the overflowing and exploding beauty that surrounds me."

Our Father created this earth and set it in continuous motion. It perpetually changes, with newness of life constantly bubbling up from within it. The Holy Spirit woos us to see creation through His heavenly eyes and not merely with the eyes of our flesh. It's the difference between seeing and operating out of the impulses of the flesh and walking in the presence of God as His Spirit reveals deep, beautiful truths. It's like suddenly going from seeing only black and white to experiencing color!

Oh, the depths and the riches of the beauty that

surrounds us and begs to be experienced in fellowship with the great I AM. In union with His heart and Spirit, we can know the incredible explosion of eternal beauty that takes place when a sin-tainted broken heart is cleansed and forever transformed by God's love. Even in death we can say, "O death, where is your victory? O death, where is your sting?" (1 Cor. 15:55). When death is swallowed up by the blood of Jesus, what's left is birth into greater, divine, eternal life. Father sees a seed falling lifelessly to the ground as the birth of a new tree, and the leaves that appear dead in the winter burst forth into a magnificent array of color and life in the spring.

I pray that the Lord opens our eyes to see His light beaming brilliantly into this world today, bringing new life and hope. May we witness what Satan meant for evil being turned around for goodness and our weaknesses being transformed to reveal God's glory.

Beloved, fellowship with your Father today so that you taste and see His goodness. The earth is filled with the beauty and glory of the Lord, and He wants you to see and experience it with Him!

> *Lord, come fill me with revelation to see as You see. As I look to You, may we revel together in Your beauty and glory, which surround me.*

Revelation Is a Gift of God

And Jesus said to him, "Blessed are you, Simon Barjona,
because flesh and blood did not reveal this to you, but
My Father who is in heaven."

—MATTHEW 16:17

WHEN I WAS in college, a friend saw a poster on my wall with Hebrews 11:1 on it: "Now faith is the substance of things hoped for, the evidence of things not seen" (NKJV). My agnostic friend asked me with sarcasm and disdain in his voice, "What does that even mean?" I looked up and read it. Though this poster of my favorite gymnast (Olga Korbut) leaping in the air had originally imparted strength and conviction to me, at that moment, during a season of doubt and walking apart from the Holy Spirit, I could not discern what it meant.

My friend and I sought to understand the scripture without consulting with the Spirit of God, and it became clear that the things of God could not be grasped through cognition alone. Understanding the Lord's ways and His Word come through communion with the Holy Spirit and receiving revelation from Him. It truly is a gift from God.

The apostle Paul wrote: "What we have received is not the spirit of the world, but the Spirit who is from God, so that we may understand what God has freely given us. This is what we speak, not in words taught us by human wisdom but in words taught by the Spirit, explaining spiritual realities with Spirit-taught words. The person without the Spirit does not accept the things that come from the Spirit of God but considers them foolishness, and cannot understand them because they are discerned only through the Spirit" (1 Cor. 2:12–14, NIV).

How ironic that the scripture we failed to understand was the verse that spoke of how we need faith, which comes through revelation, in order to comprehend and believe the Lord's Word and promises! Beloved, if you or someone you know is struggling to understand the Lord's Word, pray for the Holy Spirit to impart the gift of faith and revelation. Breakthrough is sure to follow!

> *Holy Spirit, You are my teacher. Guide me into all truth. Father, illuminate Your Word to me today. Give me a spirit of wisdom and revelation in the knowledge of You. Lord, You are the revealer of secrets. Open the eyes of my understanding, Father, and deepen my awareness of Your love for me.*

Battles Birth Blessings

We also exult in our tribulations, knowing that tribulation brings about perseverance; and perseverance, proven character; and proven character, hope; and hope does not disappoint, because the love of God has been poured out within our hearts through the Holy Spirit who was given to us.

—ROMANS 5:3–5

ONE MORNING I woke up and heard the words "Battles breathe blessings." Beloved, God wants us to think differently about the battles we face. He wants us to know that as we bring Him into our battles, they will breathe forth blessings.

Every day there is a new challenge. Even now you may be thinking of the most recent battle that has been burdening your heart. But I want you to think on Father God instead of the problem you're facing and call His Spirit into the fight.

The prophet Isaiah declared, "The steadfast of mind You will keep in perfect peace, because he trusts in You" (Isa. 26:3). This is telling us that as we call on His name throughout the day and keep our minds steadfast on the

Lord, we will experience the peace of God and the victory we desire.

Today is a new day. Yesterday's battles are gone, and new manna and revelatory words of strength are your portion for today. So call on the Lord anew, knowing that Father faithfully releases fresh manna and waters to you from His Spirit in the heavenly realms.

Beloved, be encouraged and fight the good fight. You *can* do all things through Him who strengthens you. The Spirit of God is with you, and He's bringing forth blessings from every battle as you keep your mind steadfast on Him and call on His name.

Father, thank You for causing me to triumph in Messiah Yeshua and turning my battles into blessings. Renew my strength, Holy Spirit. Help me to keep my mind steadfast on You. Your Word declares that as I trust in You, You will keep me in perfect peace. Guide me by Your hand, Lord, and lead me into victory.

Healing Companionship

> He was despised and rejected by mankind, a man of suf-
> fering, and familiar with pain. He was pierced for our
> transgressions, he was crushed for our iniquities; the
> punishment that brought us peace was on him, and by
> his wounds we are healed.
>
> —ISAIAH 53:3, 5, NIV

W HEN THE PRESSURES of life mount and the load
feels too heavy to carry, often we look to something
or someone tangible to lean in to as an escape from our
emotional weights. We may find temporary distraction
from our pain through a relationship, a TV show, work,
sex, compulsive eating, drinking alcohol, or even exces-
sive exercise.

Recently, through a dream the Holy Spirit revealed
to me another way we find escape. In the dream a sol-
dier had just returned from the battlefield. Overwhelmed
with pain and hopelessness, he went into a bar and found
another person who was experiencing the same deep distress. With a beer in hand, he told his newfound friend,
"Let's just drown our sorrows together!" This burdened sol-
dier found comfort by fellowshipping with someone who
was also experiencing pain and hopelessness. Regretfully,

the comfort found in sharing negative emotions with someone else is temporary and never life-giving.

Jesus knows the depth of human sorrows. His desire is for the heavy-laden soul to find solace and companionship in Him. He too has experienced profound emotional and physical pain. But in love He carried sorrow to the grave, destroying its power against us. Today He says: "Now that I have shared in your pain, taste of My victory over all these sorrows. Find true companionship in Me. Take comfort in My sacrificed body and blood that destroys your sin and sorrows. Receive My Word to find new hope and eternal joy. I came for *you*—to carry and defeat the weight of sin and darkness. Won't you give your burdens to Me today and let Me carry you into the light?"

Beloved, true, enduring solace cannot be found in the natural world. Find your healing comfort through companionship with the man of sorrows. This loving Shepherd will lead you out of sorrow into everlasting joy.

Thank You, Yeshua, for coming down in love to bear my sin, pain, and suffering. You are my forever companion. I lean in to You today with all my pain and sorrows. I drink of Your cup of Communion and receive the resurrection life and hope that Your blood purchased for me. This is the day that You have made, and I will rejoice and be glad in it!

The Cry of Desperation: *Come*

> The Spirit and the bride say, "Come!" And let the one who hears say, "Come!" Let the one who is thirsty come; and let the one who wishes take the free gift of the water of life.
>
> —REVELATION 22:17, NIV

THE FATHER IS calling forth from us what we don't feel we possess. He stretches us beyond our natural ways and gifts, bringing us to the end of ourselves so we become so desperate for Him that we cry, "Come, Spirit! Come, Yeshua! Come, River of Life! Flow from Your throne into my heart and soul."

When the cry of our hearts is, "Come, Lord; not my will but Yours," Father takes our hands and leads us into places where we have never walked. As we turn our eyes upward to Him, He reveals Himself as our good, mighty, and trustworthy Daddy, who loves us, equips us, and wants us to succeed.

With a wooing love, the Spirit says to us, "Come," that we would follow Him. He leads us to hidden resources, hidden wells, and hidden rivers that flow with life-giving waters. To follow His call and discover His hidden treasures, we must desire nothing of our self or of this world but seek all of Him. Through trials and tribulations our salvation in Him is worked out, and at times we will feel beaten, with nothing remaining of our old self. Cooperating with this process, we let go of the old self and cry, "Come, Lord Jesus." Our Bridegroom faithfully responds by filling the depths of our souls to make and mold us as He wills.

Precious one of the Lord, abandon yourself to Him today. Surrender your *entire* being to Him. In love and desperation, the Spirit and the bride cry to each other, "Come." Cry, "Come," and let King Jesus' ardent love arise within you. Receive new, living water in the desert places you traverse.

> *Father, come. I lay myself bare before You, empty and waiting like dead bones. Come now. Let nothing hinder what You want to do with me. Come rescue and strengthen me. Fill me with Yourself that I may arise to walk in Your ways with Your heart, mind, and will. Let nothing but Your life and love dwell within me. Eliminate everything else. Come rise up within these bones to breathe Your life. Come rise within me, Spirit of God. Raise me as You raised Yeshua from the dead that my life may become Yeshua's risen and resurrected life, for Your eternal glory. Amen.*

DAY 35

Refocus, Remember, and Rest

Again the Lord spoke to Moses, saying, "Speak to the sons of Israel, saying, 'In the seventh month on the first of the month you shall have a rest, a reminder by blowing of trumpets, a holy convocation. You shall not do any laborious work, but you shall present an offering by fire to the Lord.'"

—Leviticus 23:23–25

SOME TIME AGO the Lord spoke powerfully to me in a dream. In this dream my twenty-eight-year-old daughter was in the back seat of a limousine, resting in sheer, perfect shalom and joy. She did not know where the driver was taking her, but she trusted him and knew he would safely take her to a beautiful and blessed destination.

What struck me in this dream was the level of faith my daughter had in the driver. It was much like a child who blindly trusts her father. The dream felt so heavenly, and I knew the Lord was revealing to me how utterly trustworthy He is to safely carry us to a deeply blessed destination. I knew I must cease from striving toward the goal in Messiah and with utter abandoned faith rest in His "back seat" to enjoy a supernatural ride to reach my goals and my final, heavenly destination with Him.

Beloved, I encourage you to disconnect from your usual distractions, struggles, and busyness to refocus, remember, and *rest* in Him today. Father wants us to reflect upon and be awakened to the supernatural story playing out on earth through our lives. He wants us to focus on Him and His supernatural plans and abilities. In letting go of temporal thoughts and ambitions to seek and follow His still, small voice, we discover and experience His power and faithfulness.

Our faithful, sovereign Father has a unique, unfolding plan for each of our lives, and only He knows how to get us to our victorious, blessed destination. So rest your heart and soul in the back seat of His limousine, and let the Holy Spirit carry you to the green pastures and still waters of an abundant life!

I love You, Lord, and I sit back in trust as You take the wheel of my life. Thank You for reminding me to reflect on who You are, what You have done, and Your plans for my life. You are the same yesterday, today, and forever. With You as the driver of my life, through every storm and fire I face, I will cling to and trust in Your faithfulness to carry me to the other side and ultimately to my final, glorious destination with You.

Into a Strange and Foreign Land

We are therefore ambassadors for Messiah, as though
God were making His appeal through us. We beg you on
behalf of Messiah, be reconciled to God.

—2 CORINTHIANS 5:20, TLV

I URGE YOU TO awaken to who you are: Father's beloved
child who has been rescued from spiritual ignorance
and alienation from God your Creator through the blood
of His Son. Father has called you out of darkness and
filled you with Himself. He now sends you into a strange
and foreign land of souls who are alienated from Father's
love and in need of our Savior.

The Lord releases us into this world to be lighthouses
that draw all men into the light of Yeshua. Jesus said, "You
are the light of the world. A city set on a hill cannot be
hidden; nor does anyone light a lamp and put it under a
basket, but on the lampstand, and it gives light to all who
are in the house. Let your light shine before men in such a
way that they may see your good works, and glorify your
Father who is in heaven" (Matt. 5:14–16).

Remember that suffering souls alienated from Father
and without hope surround you. As the priests of old
made atonement for the people of Israel through the

blood of bulls and goats, so today we must bring people to God through the blood of the Lamb, who is Jesus. You are Messiah's ambassador. God is making an appeal through you to people in need of being ushered into the arms of their loving Father.

"God has given us this task of reconciling people to Him. For God was in Christ, reconciling the world to Himself, no longer counting people's sins against them. And He gave us this wonderful message of reconciliation" (2 Cor. 5:18–19, NLT). Let us go into the world as an army of believers taking God's word of hope and life across the globe. Together we are bringing heaven down to earth and leading Father's children into His loving arms!

> *Father, thank You for choosing me and loving me so much that You sent Jesus to save me, forgive me, and release me into Your arms. You bring me life and hope. Fill me afresh with Your love today. I look for doors of opportunity to take Your light and hope to those desperately in need of You. Give me Your wisdom and discernment, and equip me to walk and speak with Your heart. May my life testify of Your love and ways so others will be drawn to seek and know You as their Lord and Savior.*

Shame on Them!

Therefore do not be ashamed of the testimony of our Lord or of me His prisoner, but join with me in suffering for the gospel according to the power of God.

—2 TIMOTHY 1:8

EACH DAY, MY husband and I seek the Lord by taking time to meditate on His Word. While playing worshipful music, we cry out to our Father and listen for His subtle voice. We also study books and materials that help us grow in His truth. But just like you, we venture out and encounter a world that is not always filled with God's Spirit and truth. Many in our families, workplaces, and marketplaces do not carry our Creator's Spirit of wisdom and revelation.

One day as I was interacting with some family members, I felt a heavy oppression upon me. I silently inquired of the Lord what this was, and His Spirit showed me that it made these family members uncomfortable to hear me speak of God and how involved He is in every detail of our lives. I remembered that my earthly father believed that people who thought too frequently and expressively about Jesus as their Savior were weak and an embarrassment. The Lord revealed to me that the oppression I felt was an intimidating spirit of shame that sought to control me and my family through a fear of being rejected or emotionally abandoned.

The Lord then clearly spoke these words to me: "Shame on them, *not* shame on Me!" Revelation immediately hit me, and I repented for agreeing the times I agreed with the shame I felt for proclaiming God's love and sovereignty. I cried, "Lord, *You* are the center of the universe. And just as planets revolve around the sun, so I revolve around the Son of God, the King of kings, who was and is and is to come! I will remain in this truth and continue to speak of You in my home, my workplace, and the marketplace that *Your* name will be exalted upon the earth!"

Beloved, be keenly aware of your enemy, who lurks behind the faces of people you encounter throughout the day. He seeks to devour us with his lies and oppressive spirit. So stay alert, seek God's revelation in every situation, rebuke the devourer, and stand tall to exalt the name of Jesus, who saves and gives life!

> *Father, I reject any shame the enemy is using to oppress me. I will not be silent about who You are! Thank You for equipping me to see the devourer working through people I come in contact with and for giving me the power to take authority over him. Be exalted in my life, Lord. You always reign supreme!*

DAY 38

Look Backward and Go Forward

[Jehoshaphat prayed], "O our God, will You not judge them? For we are powerless before this great multitude who are coming against us; nor do we know what to do, but our eyes are on You."...Jehoshaphat bowed his head with his face to the ground, and all Judah and the inhabitants of Jerusalem fell down before the Lord, worshiping the Lord.

—2 CHRONICLES 20:12, 18

THOUGH THE NATURAL human reaction to foreseeable hardship is panic, fear, and anxiety, the Lord tells us time and time again, "Do not be afraid." Easier said than done, right? The story of Jehoshaphat illustrates how to face life's battles with holy confidence.

Often when we are dealing with frightening situations, we attempt to run or muster up courage, yet despite all efforts we remain paralyzed by fear. That's not what happened to Jehoshaphat. Why? Because when the Moabites and the Ammonites united to attack Judah, Jehoshaphat "turned his attention to seek the LORD" (2 Chron. 20:3) and began to recall the many things the Lord had done for the people of Israel. Rather than fearfully ruminating about all the tragic things that could happen in the future, Jehoshaphat looked back on all the times the Lord had been faithful. Remembering the times God has been faithful in the past strengthens us to exercise faith and trust Father for today and the future.

The second thing Jehoshaphat did was fall down and humbly submit himself to the almighty, glorious God, who reigns above all people, problems, and situations. Properly aligned before his Lord and with his eyes off his circumstances, Jehoshaphat looked up to worship. Worship is a lot easier when times are good, but it truly has power to transform situations in times of fear and desperation. Looking up to praise and thank God for His goodness turns our hearts away from ourselves and toward our King. Instead of focusing on bad reports, we declare the sovereignty of God and our trust in His faithfulness.

Jehoshaphat's actions moved God's heart, and He responded, "Do not fear or be dismayed because of this great multitude, for the battle is not yours but God's'" (2 Chron. 20:15). Beloved, your battle also belongs to the Lord. Whatever you are facing, follow Jehoshaphat's example and turn your fearful heart to God. Recall Father's past faithfulness, and humble yourself before Him. Release your problems to Father, and declare the power and authority of His name over every situation you face.

I praise You, Lord, for You are sovereign and faithful over my life!

Blessings Trump Curses

The Levitical priests shall step forward, for the Lord
your God has chosen them to minister and to pronounce
blessings in the name of the Lord and to decide all cases
of dispute and assault.

—DEUTERONOMY 21:5, NIV

IT SEEMS AS though another level of evil has been
released upon the earth. Pain and suffering are all
around us, and there are no doctors, kings, or presidents
who can bring healing and peace to our world. One day
my heart was so burdened by this that I cried out to the
Lord, "What about Your people? How are we to survive
and persevere through the intensity of the end times?"

As incense rises upward, so my prayer rose to our
heavenly Father. And He answered: "Though Satan
is releasing curses, I equip My people during the end
times. My equipping will keep them to the end. My
people are to bless." With His words came a great revelation: blessings trump curses. Blessings powerfully
transform people and circumstances.

As believers in Messiah Jesus, we can know that Father
receives our prayers as incense (Rev. 8:4) and has assigned
us as priests to call down blessings from His heavenly

realm. One of our assignments as His priests is to speak blessing, as we see in today's verse. The Scriptures also tell us, "Do not repay evil with evil or insult with insult. On the contrary, repay evil with blessing, because to this you were called so that you may inherit a blessing" (1 Pet. 3:9).

Beloved, I challenge you to do a Bible word search and study the word *bless*. You will be amazed to see the power of blessing revealed throughout Scripture! If you want to heal physical, emotional, and relational dysfunction, pronounce blessing. Bless your enemies in Jesus' name. Bless the ailing parts of your physical body. Bless the people you encounter throughout the day.

You have the power to bring heaven down to earth by calling Father's blessing into every situation!

> *Thank You for the privilege of being called as a priest—an intercessor—unto You. Yeshua, cleanse me and purify my heart. By Your Spirit and authority, I touch and bless this body You created. Bless my day, Lord. I move forward in Your Spirit to bless the people and situations I encounter. Bless Your people through my life. Today I move mountains by transforming curses into blessings and evil into goodness, in Jesus' name.*

Gideon, David, the Prophets, and You!

Now faith is the assurance of things hoped for, the conviction of things not seen. For by it the men of old gained approval.

—HEBREWS 11:1–2

BEFORE WORKING FULL-TIME in ministry beside my husband, I was a nurse. My heart's desire was to spend quality time with my patients, but somehow I found myself being pushed out of bedside patient care and into administrative work, and I eventually became a stressed director of nursing. At the same time, I was working hard to be the perfect mother to two school-age children and a perfect support to my husband and his congregation. But perfect was far from what I could accomplish, and the weight of my responsibilities was overwhelming.

During that busy season, I found that setting aside twenty to thirty minutes in the wee hours of the morning to hear from the Lord through His Word gave me a supernatural peace and spiritual vision for my day. Throughout the day as I continued to meditate on the power of Jesus' blood, I watched again and again as He supernaturally transformed out-of-control situations into peaceful, "in-control" situations. Father taught me that when I persevere with Him, *all* things are possible. But the only way I can live in that reality is to let Him take the wheel of every situation and look to Him for direction at every step.

Through pain, struggle, and trials of every kind, the Lord is strengthening and transforming us from the inside out so we can accomplish what He has purposed for us to do. Hebrews 11 tells of those who have gone before us— "Gideon, Barak, Samson, Jephthah, of David and Samuel and the prophets, who *by faith* conquered kingdoms, performed acts of righteousness, obtained promises, shut the mouths of lions, quenched the power of fire, escaped the edge of the sword, from weakness were made strong, became mighty in war, [and] put foreign armies to flight" (Heb. 11:32–34, emphasis added).

Beloved, an emboldened faith—assurance of Father's love and faithfulness—comes by clinging to and following the Lord through tough, seemingly out-of-control situations. Arise and persevere with the confidence that God's power is perfecting what we could never make perfect!

Father, not by power nor by might, but by Your Spirit is my life made perfect today. I trust You to do through me more than I ever thought possible. Father, take the wheel, and lead and guide me perfectly.

The Answer

Jesus said to him, "I am the way, and the truth, and the life; no one comes to the Father but through Me."

—JOHN 14:6

MANY PEOPLE SPEND their lives looking for a formula that will solve all their problems and show them the way to go in life. But just when they think they've discovered *the* answer, they find themselves again facing disappointment, pain, fear, or loneliness. They must grapple with the fact that there is no 12-step program that erases all problems. The simple yet complex answer to every question is always Jesus—He is the *way*, the *truth*, and the *life*.

Even as believers in Jesus, we may be tempted to seek specific, outlined steps that will give us the "better" life. But the truth is that the ongoing search for answers and the ups and downs of our lives *are part of the process of becoming whole in Jesus*. Our mysterious Creator says, "My thoughts are not your thoughts, neither are your ways my ways....As the heavens are higher than the earth, so are my ways higher than your ways and my thoughts than your thoughts" (Isa. 55:8–9, NIV). A 12-step program can never make a fallen, mortal man suddenly walk perfectly in the ways of his supernatural, eternal, holy Creator. Beloved, it's in our struggles that we are discovering God and journeying into wholeness.

We have been given one residing command that will faithfully equip us in reaching our goal to secure eternal life: "love the LORD your God with all your heart and with all your soul and with all your might" (Deut. 6:5). As we seek to know and love the Lord, Father provides us with what we need at each step of our journey. He does this through Jesus. Receiving revelation of Yeshua as our Messiah opens the door to relationship with our Father God. Clinging to Jesus in the ongoing journey equips us to shake off worldly thoughts and deeds in order to know the Lord as our first love. And through Jesus, the Holy Spirit releases revelation and orders each of our steps so we are drawn to love Him and carry out our assignment from Him.

> *Lord, thank You for my answer—Jesus. In each of my steps You are my way, truth, and life. In the name of Jesus, I defeat every hindrance to knowing my Father. O Holy Spirit, reveal my Father's love and ways. In Jesus' name, I rebuke every wind that comes against me. In the name of Jesus, the mountains of challenges must serve me in developing faith and trust and deepening my relationship with my Lord God Almighty!*

A KISS From God

You will seek Me and find Me when you search for Me with all your heart.

—JEREMIAH 29:13

IF YOU'VE EVER wondered who you are, hear me today: you were created by a relational God who designed you to be in relationship with Him and others. This is a fact that cannot be denied. Every deep pain and dysfunction of mankind is related to not experiencing loving, caring relationships with others.

Discovering the Jewish Jesus, the ministry my husband and I lead, travels to many of the poorest areas in the world. We have witnessed that when people are poor but in loving, caring relationships—with God, family, and others—they have joy and a drive for life. But when people are without these loving relationships, even if they are wealthy or famous, they are filled with despair.

God created us to be in relationship with Him. Only He can satisfy the deepest longings of our hearts. If you're feeling lost, purposeless, or alone, the Lord says, "Seek Me, and you will find Me." As you come to know your Creator, you will discover your identity and purpose as He defined it. And having positive relationships with others will be a natural overflow of your relationship with Him.

So receive His KISS today. Hear Him saying to you:

- *Keep* seeking intimacy with Me, making that your number one priority (Deut. 6:5).

- *I Am* is in you, giving you life and joy (Col. 1:27).

- *Sing* to praise, thank, and petition Me (Ps. 100:4; Phil. 4:6).

- *Shalom*—Let Me take control; then receive and rest in My perfect peace (John 14:27).

Beloved, there is hope. It is a new day. Receive your Creator's KISS, trusting that He is working all things together for your good.

Father, I receive and meditate on the truth of Your KISS. I choose to seek You, and I praise You for being the source of my life, hope, and joy. Father, thank You for who You are and all You have done for me. You are the same yesterday, today, and forever. So I rest in Your love and shalom—Your peace—knowing that You are in control and working every detail of my life together for my good.

DAY 43

The Longing in Your Heart

As the deer pants for streams of water, so my soul pants
for you, my God. My soul thirsts for God, for the living
God.

—PSALM 42:1–2, NIV

HAVE YOU EVER felt unsettled, as if there was a deep
hole or craving that must be filled? Our Creator
made us with these deep yearnings. But have you ever
wondered what you were yearning for?

Merriam-Webster defines a need as "something that a
person must have: something that is needed in order to
live or succeed or be happy."[1] We need food and water to
keep us alive. But we *yearn* for much more. Our hearts
are longing for love, life, identity, and purpose.

This is by design. The Father made us needy so we
would be driven to seek Him to meet these deep needs!
When my young teenage children seemed to have no
interest in the things of God, I cried out to Father on their
behalf. The Spirit responded, "Pray that they would have
the gift of hunger for Me." I replied, "Yes, Lord! If they
hunger for You, then they will seek, find, and follow You
through the rest of their lives!" I prayed this prayer, and
in the days that followed, I watched Father gift them with

a hunger to know Him. I trust that this hunger will keep them leaning in to Yeshua throughout their lives.

David the psalmist cried out to God from places of deep need. He said in Psalm 27: "Hear, O LORD, when I cry with my voice, and be gracious to me and answer me. When You said, '*Seek My face,*' my heart said to You, '*Your face, O LORD, I shall seek*'" (vv. 7–8, emphasis added). By seeking the Lord, David discovered that God is personal, is loving, and was the answer to his prayers. In Father God, David found all that he needed.

Beloved, whenever you feel lost and needy, remember that your neediness is a gift from God. Problems result if we seek to meet our needs apart from God and His wisdom. Yeshua cries out to you: "Here I am! I stand at the door and knock. If anyone hears my voice and opens the door, I will come in and eat with that person, and they with me" (Rev. 3:20, NIV).

> *Father, thank You for the gift of hunger. As the deer pants for water, so does my soul long for You. I turn away from the people and things of the world to search for You with all my heart. I delight myself in You, whom I trust.*

True Beauty

> Your beauty should not come from outward adornment,
> such as elaborate hairstyles and the wearing of gold
> jewelry or fine clothes.
>
> —1 PETER 3:3, NIV

THROUGHOUT THE SCRIPTURES we read of women who were described as beautiful and thus considered more desirable to men. Genesis 29:17 says Rachel was "beautiful of form and face," while her sister, Leah, had "weak" eyes, which resulted in Jacob seeking to marry Rachel and Leah remaining unloved (Gen. 29:31). And Scripture tells us Esther's beauty caused her to win favor with the king and be chosen as his queen.

Reading accounts such as these has caused some women, myself included at one time, to think that without some form of physical beauty, rejection and loneliness would be our lot. Men too may read scriptures about Abraham and Solomon gaining great wealth or Samson having great strength and think their value comes from being strong, handsome, or prosperous.

But in Jeremiah 9:23–24 the Lord speaks a different word to us. He tells us not to boast of wisdom, might, and riches but to boast that we know the One who bestows loving-kindness, justice, and righteousness. And in 1 Peter 3:3 we find that our beauty should not come from outer adornment. "Rather, it should be that of your inner self, the unfading beauty of a gentle and quiet spirit, which is of great worth in God's sight. For this is the way the holy women of the past who put their hope in God used to adorn themselves" (1 Pet. 3:4–5, NIV).

Beloved, to discover true, lasting strength and beauty, reject the idea that your identity, value, and lot in life result from your outward appearance and material success. The Lord says today, "Do not fear rejection and failure, but pursue Me." You have been bought with the blood of Jesus, and the Lord will not allow you to fail. He will bless you, keep you, and make His beautiful face to shine upon you. As you pursue God to receive Father's love and beauty, you will most assuredly glow with His glory and strength and speak with His profound wisdom.

Holy Spirit, shepherd me. Lead me even in the care of my body and what to wear each day. You are the master artist, who created me perfectly. So now, Father, come fill me with Your love and adorn me with Your Spirit so that Your glory, power, and goodness shine from me into this world.

Unlock the Mystery

That is, the mystery which has been hidden from the past ages and generations, but has now been manifested to His saints, to whom God willed to make known what is the riches of the glory of this mystery among the Gentiles, which is Christ in you, the hope of glory.

—COLOSSIANS 1:26–27, EMPHASIS ADDED

GOD'S WORD IS filled with intrigue and can seem like a mystery to be solved. Who is this One who created all things, including you and me? How does He operate? What are His motives, and how do I fit into His plan?

When approached as a book of knowledge, the Scriptures often are misunderstood and leave people confused. But when approached as a mystery to be solved *through the Spirit of the author*, the Bible imparts a life-giving revelation of truth into our inner man and reveals the God and Creator of all, whose deepest desire is for connection and relationship with the people He created.

From beginning to end, God's Word is a love story written with you and me in mind. In Colossians, Paul shares that our Messiah Jesus came in Father's love to take the blindfolds off our fallen, mortal eyes so we could see and experience the deepest, most satisfying relationship there is—*having the Spirit of God living within our mortal bodies!*

When you receive Jesus, you also receive the Father and the Spirit into your heart and soul, bringing you into oneness in spirit with the Creator. This is how it feels to experience love at its deepest level. So I encourage you to read and search the Scriptures with the Spirit of the author as your guide. Then you will discover what it means to have *Christ in you, the hope of glory!*

Father, thank You for loving me and for expressing Your love for me through Your Word. Holy Spirit, as I read Your Word, come bring heavenly revelation that I may deeply know the truth of God, the love of my Father, and the way of Jesus. Father, I want to experience intimacy with You. Remove every hindrance so I can walk in the full reality of "Christ in me, the hope of glory"!

Your Life Is a Diamond

The joy of the Lord is your strength.

—NEHEMIAH 8:10

THE WORD OF God tells us the joy of the Lord is our strength. But we cannot experience this joy until we let go of our old paradigm to see life from *His* paradigm. Every day we battle to gain His perspective, let go of our own, and then think and act in accordance with His ways.

More than anything, the Lord wants you to know that your matchless Creator made you perfectly *just as you are*. He gave you life as a gift of love to you, Himself, and this world. *Selah*, think on that for a moment. Let go of any negative views you have of yourself. See Yeshua's blood washing away all your sin-stained impressions of who you are. You are God's treasured creation, a diamond created for His love and light to pass through. As you receive His perfect forgiveness and love into your heart, you can release this divine love back to Him and into this world. This is how we experience *true* joy.

To discover the brilliant, shimmering beauty of your diamond today, begin to look at your trials and tribulations differently. Rebuke the fears they trigger, and see that these battles propel you into the arms of your Maker. Nothing else is more important than for you to look to Him as your Daddy, Creator, and Savior, seeking everything you need from His loving arms. Deep brokenness will cause you to seek your Father's face and relinquish your problems to Jesus at the cross.

Philippians 4:6 reveals there's power when we pray with thanksgiving. Thank Him for Jesus, for His faithfulness in the past, and for revealing the next step to take. When we place our lives in Father's hands, every "thorn in the flesh" (2 Cor. 12:7) causes us not to rely upon ourselves but to look to God to receive *His* love and learn His ways. Nothing else can bring *true* joy.

You are Father's treasured diamond created to receive His unconditional love. Let His living, active love and light shine through you back to Him and into this world. Receiving His love and releasing it back to Him and others is true joy—the joy of the Lord that is your strength!

> *Thank You, Lord, for creating me perfectly. I am Your diamond, cleansed and receiving Your love and light. Fill me afresh with Your Spirit so I can see trials and tribulations as You see them. I love You, trust You, and release Your unconditional love to others today, for I am Your diamond reflecting Your glory.*

Love Well

I pray that you, being rooted and established in love, may have power, together with all the Lord's holy people, to grasp how wide and long and high and deep is the love of Christ.

—EPHESIANS 3:17–18, NIV

SEVERAL YEARS AGO as I was seeking the Holy Spirit for revelation of His heart and vision for the coming year, I strongly sensed Him saying to me, "Love well."

After He spoke those profound words to me, the Spirit of God led me to Song of Solomon 2:14: "My dove in the clefts of the rock…show me your face, let me hear your voice; for your voice is sweet, and your face is lovely" (NIV). He seemed to be saying, "Talk to Me out loud. I created your vocal cords so I could hear the beautiful sound of your voice. Tell Me what you are thinking. Seek My heart concerning every detail of your life."

Loving involves both knowing someone and being known. So to love well, we must first receive Yeshua's love and then express our thoughts to Him. As we practice talking to God each day, we will experience His presence, discern His voice, and see Him respond.

Loving well also includes loving other believers in

Jesus. This is very challenging because the church consists entirely of imperfect people! Christians get judged harshly because some think that once we are saved, we instantly no longer sin. This is far from the truth. The difference between nonbelievers and followers of Messiah is that believers are saved by Jesus' blood and our names are written in the Book of Life. We have a new heart that seeks to know the Lord and be transformed from the inside out, but transformation takes a lifetime. Loving well as a follower of Messiah must include a process of receiving Father's mercy, grace, and unconditional love and then releasing this love to others.

Finally, to love well, we must not only receive Father's love but also release this profound love to a lost world. Life can be extremely stressful, and people around us are experiencing deep fear, rejection, loneliness, and self-condemnation. Living without the knowledge of Father God results in abrasive, defensive, and polarizing behaviors. Father is calling us to release His unconditional love to those around us so they can find peace in Him.

Beloved, let's love well and build the kingdom of God!

Yeshua, I open my broken heart and receive the healing balm of Your unconditional love. Use me today to release this life-transforming love to others.

Turn Your Gaze Toward Heaven

Therefore if you have been raised up with Christ, keep seeking the things above, where Christ is, seated at the right hand of God. Set your mind on the things above, not on the things that are on earth.

—COLOSSIANS 3:1–2

WARRIOR FOR MESSIAH, be assured of this today: as you fight the good fight—clinging to Father God, depending on Him, and trusting that Jesus' blood has destroyed the power of sin and darkness—you *will* be victorious. Rest in Jesus, for today's victory won't come from striving for perfection. Fleshly striving merely causes us to spin our wheels and dig a deeper hole of frustration. What determines success is a steadfast heart that keeps pressing in to Yeshua against every headwind.

As we draw closer to Jesus' return, the challenges are coming one after another, seemingly more fiercely and fervently than ever before. The enemy relentlessly attacks our minds with lying, deceptive thoughts that seek to overwhelm us with fear, anxiety, or depression. The mind is complex, and each day fields a multitude of thoughts, both conscious and unconscious. Added to these incessant thoughts are surroundings that bombard us with eye-catching distractions. Our constant battle is to stay focused on the truth that reigns from above, because Satan knows that if he can take our eyes off our almighty Father, we will continually strike out in life.

So be steadfast today, keeping your gaze fixed toward heaven and your heart in tune with Father God. Let the sensation of oppression trigger you to step back from the busyness of life and spend time talking to your compass, the Holy Spirit. Declare God's Word and call on His Spirit to fill you, go before you, and direct you. As you do, you will find that His love will steer you in the right direction. As you stay sensitive and catch the wind of His Spirit, He will lead you safely to your destination in Him.

And if you feel overwhelmed or as if you've gone off course, rejoice. You are in a perfect position to humbly call upon the Lord and be filled with the One who will redirect your path and lead you to victory! Treasured one, Father God believes in your progress, and He sees you as perfect in His Son. Just keep turning your gaze toward your heavenly Father.

In the name of Jesus, I rebuke the thoughts and distractions that keep me from connecting with You, Father. I fix my eyes on You, the author and perfecter of my faith. I run my race to the end for Your glory!

Sharp and Strong

Iron sharpens iron, so one man sharpens another.
—Proverbs 27:17

IS THERE SOMEONE in your life who feels like a thorn in your flesh? Perhaps it is someone in your congregation or your workplace, a family member, or possibly even your spouse. Because of this "thorn," do you avoid gathering with other believers or dodge seeing people who could cause further pain? If so, you are not alone, but it is important to understand that in life conflict is to be expected and not something we should run from.

Being created in the image of our relational God, we crave relationship. Ideally His love is to flow through us to others. However, there is an unholy spirit that opposes God's flow of love and relationship, and it actually works to separate us from God and others. The Word tells us that we wrestle not against flesh and blood but against spiritual forces of wickedness (Eph. 6:12). When words are spoken that wound us, threaten our self-esteem, or cause us to fear or become angry, we know that the spiritual forces of wickedness are at work. Yet what Satan means for evil, God works for our good.

Proverbs speaks of one person sharpening another. Relationships that trigger pain or discomfort can actually sharpen us as individuals. The key to handling painful relationships is to see them with spiritual eyes. Rebuke Satan's spirit of division, humbly lay down all pride, pray for your enemies to be moved by Yeshua's heart, and look to the Father to receive and walk in His truth. Through prayer, revelation, repentance, forgiveness, and Father's healing love, our challenging relationships can make us sharper, wiser, and filled with a new love and peace.

Yeshua wants to impart His healing love and security into every one of our relationships. So today, face that "thorn" in your flesh. Humbly take your relationships to the Lord to receive correction when needed and to discover Father's unconditional love that heals and transforms us, as iron sharpens iron!

Father, use the difficult people and situations in my life to make me more like You. I repent of my pride and choose to face whatever fears and hurt I may be holding in my heart. Give me revelation so I can see when Satan is at work, and take authority over the demonic forces that seek to wound and divide. Heal me with Your love, Abba Father, and sharpen me through my relationships with others.

Messengers for Messiah Moving Mountains

> For the body is not one member, but many....If the whole body were an eye, where would the hearing be? If the whole were hearing, where would the sense of smell be? But now God has placed the members, each one of them, in the body, just as He desired.
>
> —1 Corinthians 12:14, 17–18

For more than thirty years, my husband and I have been leading Discovering the Jewish Jesus and taking the gospel to people around the world. Although we know God has anointed us to do this work, we could not have accomplished all we have if not for those who have faithfully supported us.

Beloved of God, whether you are holding the microphone, proclaiming the gospel, or supporting others who are doing so, you are making a difference. By serving in whatever way God has called you, the Word of the Lord is going forth as a sharp, double-edged sword and penetrating darkened minds and closed hearts. It is shattering Satan's strongholds and building the Lord's eternal kingdom. Together we are Yeshua's body on earth moving mountains. Souls are being set free because of each person's faithfulness to do what God is calling them to do.

My prayer for you today echoes the words of the apostle Paul in Ephesians 3:14–19: "For this reason I bow my knees before the Father, from whom every family in heaven and on earth derives its name, that He would grant you, according to the riches of His glory, to be strengthened with power through His Spirit in the inner man, so that Christ may dwell in your hearts through faith; and that you, being rooted and grounded in love, may be able to comprehend with all the saints what is the breadth and length and height and depth, and to know the love of Christ which surpasses knowledge, that you may be filled up to all the fullness of God."

No matter where the Lord has placed you, whether in a position of prominence or behind the scenes, as you obey His leading in your life, He will use you to move mountains.

> *Father, thank You for the important part You have given me to play in Your body. Thank You for anointing me with Your Spirit in such unique ways. May I never become jealous of someone else's gift or calling, for You've created me perfectly to do what only I can do on earth and for such a time as this. Lord, sharpen my gifts so they are used to build love, unity, and Your kingdom.*

NOTES

1. *Merriam-Webster*, s.v. "need," accessed May 29, 2020, https://www.merriam-webster.com/dictionary/need.

ABOUT THE AUTHOR

CYNTHIA SCHNEIDER AND her husband, Rabbi Kirt A. Schneider, lead Discovering the Jewish Jesus, an international outreach and popular television broadcast. Over the last thirty years, Cynthia has traveled and pastored with her husband, ministering God's love and healing to His people. Together they deliver God's fresh, fire-filled words via television and numerous media outlets, imparting divine faith, hope, and love of the Father to His children.

Rabbi and Cynthia Schneider host the international television broadcast *Discovering the Jewish Jesus*, which can be seen seven days a week in more than one hundred million homes in the United States and approximately two hundred nations worldwide. Viewers tune in regularly as Rabbi Schneider shows with exceptional clarity how the Old and New Testaments connect and how Jesus completes the unfolding plan of God. For a list of times and stations that broadcast *Discovering the Jewish Jesus* in your area, visit *www.DiscoveringTheJewishJesus.com* and click on the "Ways to Watch" tab.

Cynthia and her husband live in Ohio and have two married daughters and five grandchildren.

www.DiscoveringTheJewishJesus.com

DISCOVERING THE JEWISH JESUS

CONNECT WITH RABBI SCHNEIDER

www.DiscoveringTheJewishJesus.com

 www.facebook.com/rabbischneider

 @RabbiSchneider

 @discoveringthejewishjesus

 / Discovering the Jewish Jesus with Rabbi Schneider